A WEALTH OF INFORMATION!

"EALTH!

EASY TO FOLLOW!

A REALISTIC APPROACH!

A MUST READ!

PRAISE FOR LARRYETTE KYLE DEBOSE

"Larryette, you're a genius! You created a text that contains **a wealth of information**. I don't care if you live in a penthouse or an out house—this book will find a way to place a few extra bucks into your pocket."
— Dennis Kimbro, author, *Think & Grow Rich: A Black Choice*

"Ms. DeBose by writing this book demonstrates that she **understands the significance of economic development in the African-American community** in general, and how it effects the 'Black Family' in particular. This completely supports NCNW's philosophy of building economically through entrepreneurship. **Great Job!**"
— Dr. Dorothy I. Height, **President, National Council of Negro Women**

"Larryette Kyle DeBose's practical, no-nonsense book, *The African-American Guide to Real Estate Investing*, is a must-read for anyone serious about property investing. In it, she lays out a blueprint for wealth creation that's not only easy-to-follow, but practical and doable—the rest is up to you!"
— Cynthia Franklin, Editor, *The KIP Business Report*

"Investing in Real Estate can be a **means to wealth**, and real estate investor **DeBose shows us how**…short-term plans, laying the groundwork, finding funding and marketing investment properties."

 —Ann Burns, Editor, *Library Journal*

"As I state in my books, you have to get real about real estate as an investment. Larryette Kyle DeBose **illustrates how to get started in the real estate market place** in 30 days! Use this guide to assess your keys to real estate investing success."

 —Jesse B. Brown, Financial Guru, President/CEO-Krystal
  Investment Management, Author, *Pay Yourself First, The African American Guide to Financial Success & Security, 101 Real Money Questions – The African-American Financial Question & Answer Book* and *Invest in the Dream*

"Larryette's book offers a no hype **realistic approach** to the topic of real estate investing. She shares her many years of wisdom and experience by illustrating an **easy to follow step-by-step system.** Great job!"

 —Theresa Hall, Past President, Georgia Real Estate Investors
  Association

The African-American Guide To Real Estate Investing

$30,000 in 30 Days

The Handbook & Guide Through Your First
Real Estate Deal...and Beyond

Larryette Kyle DeBose

Amber Books

Phoenix
New York   Los Angeles

The African-American Guide To Real Estate Investing
$30,000 in 30 Days
The Handbook & Guide Through Your First Real Estate Deal...and Beyond

By Larryette Kyle DeBose

Published by:
Amber Books
A Division of Amber Communications Group, Inc.
1334 East Chandler Boulevard, Suite 5-D67
Phoenix, AZ 85048
amberbk@aol.com
WWW.AMBERBOOKS.COM

Tony Rose, Publisher/Editorial Director   Samuel P. Peabody, Associate Publisher
Yvonne Rose, Senior Editor   The Printed Page, Interior & Cover Design
Jarmell J. Boyd-Sims, Editor

Library of Congress Cataloging-in-Publication Data

DeBose, Larryette Kyle..
    The African-American guide to real estate investing : $30,000 in 30 days : the handbook
& guide through your first real estate deal-- and beyond / by Larryette Kyle DeBose.
       p. cm.
    Includes index.
    ISBN 0-9727519-6-3
    1. Real estate investment--United States. 2. African Americans--Finance, Personal. I.
Title.

HD255.D43 2004
332.63'24'08996073--dc22

                                                              2004045789

Dedicated **TO**

MUDIA *my grandmother*
who was on this earth for 91 years till 2001.
She was definitely a black woman ahead of her time.
She lived thru the great Depression and in spite of it
was a business owner, a real estate investor
IN the South, IN the '30s
She was also the youngest of two girls
having16 older brothers
She was a Wife, Mother, Sister and Aunt par excellence

Was she perfect? Absolutely Not,
but she loved me unconditionally and
She supported me
Whatever I wanted to do,
Wherever I wanted to go,

Whatever I wanted to be.

She is there for me and lights my way

THANKS·MUDIA

Acknowledgments

There are so many people to thank, every person situation and circumstance in my life has led to the creation of this book. I must first acknowledge my Higher Power, as taught to me by the Late Rev O.C. Smith and His wife Robie. Next I want to thank my son Aaron Short, for his daily encouragement love and support. He totally believed in this project and his Mom.

I've had several mentors along my path I would like to thank them all; but, I'll name only those few who took me under their wing at some point, and taught me either about business, real estate or life in general: Dr. Dorothy I. Height, Senator Mdiniso, Ruth Soumah, Robert Allen and Louis Brown.

I was also heavily influenced by the following great authors: Dr. John Aiken, Melody Beatie, Les Brown, W.E.B.DuBois, DR William Danko/Dr. Thomas Stanley, Kahlil Gibran, Mark Victor Hanson, Rev Ike, Dr. Dennis Kimbro, Robert Kiyosaki, Dr. Bernice Lido, Dr. JSM Matsebula, Terry McMillan, Barbara Sher, Jose Silva, and Susan L Taylor; to name only a few.

I must also acknowledge the strong black female role models in my life, who taught me the values and character traits that put me on the road to achievement, my mother Beatrice Hayes, my aunt Emelda Tolder and my godmother the late Florence Edmonds.

My brothers Norman and Chuckie, my sister Sharon, my lifelong friend Gwen Evans and my second family, my tennis team of ten years, all provided a constant cheering section during this project...and I want to say thanks.

One other person that I wish to acknowledge is Ms. Stacie Moore who provided transcription services, and that was no easy task.
Last but not least I want to thank Tony and Yvonne Rose for believing in an unknown, unpublished writer and for providing constant encouragement, technical services, and support, as needed.
—L K DeBose

About the Author

Larryette Kyle DeBose has over 22 years of real estate experience, including: holding Real Estate licenses in four states and selling commercial business properties. For more than fifteen years Ms. DeBose has been actively involved in real estate investing—tax properties, rehabs, foreclosures, restorations, rentals, and discounted notes.

Prior to her real estate career, Ms. Debose gained extensive experience as co-owner in a business development/ incubator center located in Beverly Hills, California, where she procured, negotiated and administered government transcription contracts for the business center.

She has also traveled extensively over four continents and lived in Swaziland Southern Africa for five years.

Larryette Kyle DeBose has a Masters Degree in Public Administration (MPA) from the University of Southern California. Ms. DeBose currently resides in Stone Mountain, Georgia and has one son.

Contents

Introduction

If you're reading this book or even perusing it, you're obviously expressing an interest in transforming your life by increasing your financial wealth. You have also obviously decided that investing in real estate is the vehicle that you prefer to use.

For purposes of this book wealth is defined in monetary terms where "your assets (including your cash flow) continue to be greater than your liabilities on a long-term basis". In other words, you are debt free and have enough cash flow coming in each month to pay all of your bills and have enough left over to invest so that your money starts working for you instead of you working for your money.

If you're not already in this position you'll have to have what is called a "paradigm shift". You must change your thinking. It can be done little by little, step-by-step.

Every accomplishment, great or small, began as a thought in someone's mind.

First, we will start by planting the seeds of change. You must begin seeing possibilities You must stop focusing on "why you don't have enough money to pay this or that or the other, but rather how you can create...yes, I said create...more sources of income". I did not say the "paradigm shift" would be easy, but it is necessary if you're serious about changing your wealth picture. This is just one more form of faith.

At this point, if you don't feel that you can even be open to the possibilities, then I suggest you close this book right now and pick up the classifieds, find a second or third job and see if that works for you.

But, on the other hand if you can at least say well let me see where this leads me then the seeds have been successfully planted, and by the time you're finished reading this book you will begin the harvest.

Most of us are familiar with the definition of insanity which is "doing the same old thing and expecting different results". If you're not where you want to be in life now, and you continue doing what you're doing now, you will continue not being where you want to be in life.

In essence, you're going to have to stretch your mind and probably change some of your existing beliefs if you're truly serious about making it in this business.

You literally cannot afford this kind of thinking if you want to accomplish your dreams in life.

There have been that many studies on why people succeed and fail in business. Some of the more recent studies have dealt with millionaires as described in books like *Think and Grow Rich: A Black Choice* by Dennis Kimbro. After all is said and done it boils down to the why do you want to have financial wealth? What is it you really want? If there's not a strong enough why you probably won't do what it takes to get it.

That's why this book incorporates questions that help people explore the why. Oddly enough if people don't have a strong enough why they won't take the time to even answer the questions.

The style of this book makes the subject of real estate investing simple and fun. In some cases this book relates and compares everyday activities that people already do to use the skill sets necessary to do real estate investing; thus, showing the similarities in the skills that they already have and need to do this business.

Then, through an additional series of questions people can identify exactly what they want for themselves and how close they are to accomplishing those goals.

The development of real estate investing is a highly creative business because each transaction is unique. Each seller, buyer, mortgage broker, appraiser, closing attorney, etc has his/her own personality and style. To be successful in this business you must use your skills to orchestrate all of the different elements of a transaction.

Buying properties is a very emotional experience, however. When we, as African Americans, purchase our first home it usually takes months and sometimes years to decide on just the right house. The real estate investment business is just the opposite. You must take your emotions out of the equation and disconnect your home buying experience from your real estate investment buying experience. You must look at purchasing any real estate investment as just another functional commodity, such as a suit or car.

I suggest that you already have bought your own home before you start the real estate investment business so that you're not looking at every deal as a possibility for you yourself to live in. You can do real estate investing without owning your own home, but it tends to cloud your objectivity. Whereas, buying your own home, can be an emotional decision, purchasing any investment property must be a business decision.

This book is geared toward the people who have a desire to invest but have not yet made up their minds to use real estate as a major investment tool. Some of you have seen or heard horror stories about real estate investing, particularly real estate rentals. Others of you believe you don't have the money, time experience, etc., to do a real estate investing business.

During one of the first real estate investment courses that I ever attended the question was asked what is the one characteristic a person needs to do this business? People guessed everything from money, education and knowledge, to contacts to experience. The answer was "GUTS" and I have since turned the word into an acronym (GUTS) *Get Up and Tackle Something,* which we will be using throughout this book.

This book builds on your current life skills and enhances the technical knowledge that creates the perfect marriage between creativity and the practical, which enhances us as African-Americans and as real estate investors.

Our African-American heritage lends to some special skills as real estate investing professionals One such skill is our industriousness. Historically, many years ago our ancestors lives depended on how industrious they were. I believe those skills are brought forward, as well as other such characteristics, like, caretaking in the sense of being nurturing. Honesty, integrity and hard work are other skills that African Americans are noted for historically.

We must also remember that economics, not race, is oftentimes the key factor in African Americans getting ahead. When we look at examples like Madame C. J. Walker who lived on the Hudson River in New York City in the 1800s and Nat King Cole, who lived in the heart of Bel Air in the late '30s and early 40s, we see examples of individuals who had the money, the economics to choose where they lived even during times of major racial segregation in our country.

This book presents real-life examples you can follow, and, unlike other books it speaks about the good, the bad, and the ugly showing however, in the long run the good far outweighs the bad and the ugly in the real estate investing business.

—L.K. DeBose

"You can have it all. You just can't have it all at one time."
—Oprah Winfrey

Chapter 1

So...You Want to Own a Successful Real Estate Investment Business!

Why Start a Real Estate Investment Business?

You should go into real estate investing, as a business, for two reasons: 1) to make money and 2) to provide an excellent product or service to a targeted market. If you accomplish the second reason, the first reason will automatically follow.

So, if you are one of those people who are willing to do now, what other people are unwilling to do, then later you'll be able to do what you want to do, while other people are doing what they have to do, to survive.

If you want to be successful in your Real Estate Investment Business, you must show a commitment of time and money. Remember, PEOPLE DO THEIR PRIORITIES. The only commodity in the universe that you cannot create is TIME, therefore you should guard it with your life, and not allow anyone to rob you of it.

Setting Up Your Real Estate System

You should structure your Real Estate Investment Business properly from the very beginning, so you can reap the benefits now, and not suffer negative consequences later. In the beginning, your Real Estate Investment Business' structure does not need to be sophisticated.

I strongly suggest that as you begin, to set up a separate bank account for your business only. You can usually start one for as little as $100.

A separate account will enable you to maintain separate books and records, which will make it much easier to pay taxes.

As part of setting up your Real Estate Investment Business, you'll need to hire your accountant and/or attorney. You can either retain them for specific services or see them whenever necessary—maybe once or twice a year.

Spend the money up front, and get set up right. In the long-run, you'll save both time and money

Just A Precaution!

One of the biggest mistakes that small business owners make, is not setting up their financial books and records, or paying taxes.

You should also designate and set up your office space, even if it is in your home. To get started, you will need a desk, telephone, fax machine, computer and /or word processor, and a file cabinet.

Get On the Road to Wealth!!

The only way to *build* wealth, is to grow your income through investing. This brings us to the four cornerstones that maintain the foundation of building wealth:

Cornerstone 1: A Defined Income Stream. Income can be acquired in many ways. But, once you've read this guide and put your plan into action, your income will come primarily through your Real Estate Investment Business.

Cornerstone 2: Paid Debt. As a credit driven society, this is one of the most difficult tasks for Americans to accomplish. The only way to pay off debt is to cut up the credit cards, and as Financial Guru Jesse Brown puts it: "Live below your means, and invest the rest."

Cornerstone 3: Putting Aside 10 Percent. Get into the habit of saving a minimum of 10 percent of your income, even while you are paying off your debt. So, why not have a nest egg to fall back on, or invest in your Real Estate Investment Business?

Cornerstone 4: Small Investments: Make small investments such as opening a mutual fund account. You can do this for as little as $25. You can also make small investments in tax certificates, secured by real estate. In addition, you can purchase real estate using your IRA account (talk to your tax accountant, or your attorney to learn how).

Take Action!

No one has ever achieved wealth without taking CALCULATED RISKS. None of us are smart enough to acquire wealth without making some mistakes. This is how you learn. In order to accomplish great things, you must take action.

Starting Your Real Estate Investment Business

There are three easy steps for beginning your real estate investment business. You generally start out with limited time and resources, therefore step 1 is the critical step:

Step 1: Choosing an area of real estate in which to focus

This is probably the most difficult job for the beginning real estate investor. Because there are hundreds of ways to make a lot of money in the real estate investment business, it's hard to choose when you know very little about any of them.

Below is a list of several possible areas to begin your real estate investment business, as well as suggestions of the easiest, most affordable, and the most profitable ways to get started. Here is a brief description of some real estate fields you might consider specializing in:

▼ **Adult Congregate Living Facilities**—Purchase and operate group homes for senior assisted living, mentally challenged, halfway houses for adult offenders, temporary housing for the homeless etc. The government will provide funding for many of these living arrangements.

▼ **Auctions**—Purchase properties only through private and government auctions, such as tax sales, large government obsolete properties like post offices and schools. These properties are often bought by investors to do large loft projects.

▼ **Collecting Liens & Judgments**—This business requires learning simple steps for locating information and filing forms to assist people that have been awarded judgments against real property for collection. You are paid by getting a commission on what you collect.

▼ **Commercial Property**—Purchasing commercial properties, such as strip malls, shopping Centers, warehouses, restaurants, retail stores etc. These are very lucrative projects, but require experience, and usually a large upfront investment.

▼ **Direct Marketing Real Estate**—Business that just creates and distributes marketing materials to sell real estate. Companies such as "Buy Owner" is an excellent example.

▼ **Discounted Paper Buying and selling**—Discounted paper is also known as " Discounted Notes". When purchasing the note you are only purchasing the instrument that secures the property, not the property itself. Basically you are just buying the loan on the property.

▼ **Foreclosure Specialist**—Foreclosures are wholesale or discounted properties generally, but the lender has already received the property back through a sale on the courthouse steps. Specialists in this area of real estate get very good deals and the property has no title problems and no tenants.

▼ **Lease Options**—Buying properties with lease options gives the buyer the right to purchase the property at a later date under certain terms and conditions. The buyer has control of the property during the option period. The other part to complete the option is the lease, which is a regular rental agreement sometimes allowing for funds to be allocated toward the option.

▼ **Mobile Homes—Purchase and Sale** or mobile home parks. The mobile parks are where you rent spaces for mobile home owners.

▼ **Mortgage Broker—**Works on funding side of the real estate business securing loans for buyers from various lenders.

▼ **Mortgage Reduction Program—**Works with homeowners to assist them in mortgage payment arrangements that cut years off their current loan. Reviews their tax and mortgage payments to make sure they are not overpaying.

▼ **Multi-family Units—**Purchase of 5 or more units for rental income or for resale. A benefit of multi-units is that if one unit is vacant, the other 3 units can still pay the note.

▼ **Options—**It is an agreement that allows the buyer to purchase a piece of property under specific terms and conditions, and is binding on the seller, but not the buyer. This instrument is used often in large real estate transactions, such as shopping centers, hotels, large tracts of land etc.

▼ **Property Management—**Individuals or companies that handle the day to day operations of pieces of rented real estate. Property managers find tenants, evict tenants, handle the internal and external maintenance, pay the notes and prepare reports for the owners.

▼ **Real Estate Agent—**Person licensed by the state, in which they practice, to assist people in the purchase and sale of their property for a commission.

▼ **Rehabber—**Person that purchases property at a deep discount and repairs and then sells it for a profit, or rents it for income.

▼ **Rental Units buyers**(1-4 family)—Person that usually purchases duplexes, triplexes or quadraplexes and rents them for income. They prefer the smaller multis.

▼ **Retailing Houses**—Houses sold for market value, real estate agents sell most of their listings retail, and rehabbers sell their properties for full value after they have been repaired.

▼ **Wholesaling Houses**—Purchase properties at a deep discount and resell them after doing minor repairs or no repairs at a discount to another investor.

Lease Options, Wholesaling, and Collection of Judgments and Liens are the most profitable areas to start your Real Estate Investment Business. They also require the shortest learning curve, the least amount of money to start; and you could literally be making a lot more money within the first month.

Step 2. Learning the business basics

New investors can learn the basics of real estate investing by reading real estate books, and/or attending seminars, and classes. However, the best way to reduce the learning curve, is to hook up with someone you trust, who is also a real estate business investor. This is where real estate investment associations come in to play.

Take Note!

You can attend real estate association meetings, and trade what is called "sweat equity". This means, you do the legwork of locating properties for an experienced investor, and in return, they will train you, or sometimes even partner with you on your first deals.

Step 3. Using your "GUTS" (Get Up and Tackle Something)

Take action! You must use your "GUTS"! Quite frankly, this is where many beginners get stumped. They get into what we call the "paralysis of analysis" syndrome; meaning, beginners feel they need to know all there is to know, before making an offer. Unfortunately, the result is that they do nothing.

The Real Estate Investment Business requires continued learning, and even the most experienced investors realize that there's always more to learn. So, do your "due diligence", crunch your numbers, take a calculated risk, and invest. We will guide you in how to keep your losses to a minimum, but you can't lose what you don't risk.

Create Your Criteria

As a beginner, the first thing you will need to do before looking for property to invest in, is to create a set of criteria. It may be a bit difficult to know exactly what you want, but you can decide how much money you would like to make *per deal.*

You've probably seen or heard this phrase: Real estate investing is IDEAL because it provides the following:

> I—Income
> D—Depreciation
> E—Equity
> A—Appreciation
> L—Leverage

These are the only two things you need to know in order to make money in real estate investing:

> 1. What is the value of the property?
> 2. What is the true cost to purchase the property?

Once you determine these two things, you will know how much profit you can make in any real estate deal. But where do you find the real estate? This is by far, the most frequently asked question. There are hundreds of thousands of properties in the marketplace, and given the right set of circumstances, they can all become successful real estate transactions.

The question should be, how do you know *when* to purchase a property? You should always compare it to other similar real estate. This can be done in three primary ways:

1. Hire a certified appraiser to do an appraisal. They will find comparable sales for the area usually within a six-month period of time, then compile a detailed report (cost may range from $75 to $500).

2. Have a Realtor do what is called a comparative sales report. The Realtor will compile a list of all the singular sales in a specific area, usually within the last six months to a year. They will usually do this service for free.

3. You can also do a comparable yourself by:

   Purchasing a Local or Nationwide Database Program that will provide you with sales data information.

   Surfing the Internet. Property sales and property tax information is a matter of public record. There are several sites that will provide property value information across the country. For starters, do a search, using keyword "Real Estate" to find real estate information in your local area. But, if the information is not available on the Internet, you can go down to your local county courthouse and look up the sales, and property tax records using a street address.

Here's a Great List of Real Estate Sites to help you locate foreclosures in your area:

www.hud.gov/homes	(Housing and Urban Development-HUD)
www.mortgagecontent.net	(Fannie Mae)
www.homesteps.com	(Freddie Mac)
www.treas.gov/auctions/irs	(Internal revenue service -IRS)
www.2.fdic.gov/drrore	(Federal Deposit Insurance Corp - FDIC)
Http://app1.sba.gov/pfsales	(SBA)
www.bargain.com	(Find foreclosure)
www.ucma.com	(Nationwide foreclosure help)
www.foreclosurefile.com	(Real Estate investor opportunities)
www.realtytrac.com	(Find foreclosed homes- nationwide)
www.reozone.com	(Foreclosed real estate homes)
www.azhud.com	(Free foreclosure information)

Some of these site offer a free trial but will charge a fee for their services.

Joining your Local Real Estate Association. You can usually gain access to databases for free, or for a nominal fee.

FYI: 10 Reasons Why You Should Join Your Local Real Estate Investors Group

1. It is one of the best places to *find great deals.*

2. You can *meet veteran investors* doing exactly what you want to do and can pick their brains, usually their very cooperative.

3. You can easily *find a mentor or coach* at these gatherings.

4. You *can find investors to partner with* and do deals.

5. Many associations *offer their members resources*, such as membership to credit unions, health plans, discount prices for various purchases for services and goods.

6. You *can locate contractors* involved in every disciple, such as painters, carpenters, roofers, electricians etc.

7. You can *find real estate professionals* from every area, such as lawyers, accountants, appraisers, realtors, mortgage lenders, everyone you'll need to develop you real estate support "Dream Team".

8. You *can join* smaller groups usually called *"sub-groups"*, that deal specifically with the area of real estate that you are interested in.

9. You *can participate in effecting legislation* that effects real estate, oftentimes, members are asked to give testimony or write or call their representatives to express their viewpoints. You will obtain updated information on laws that effect real estate investing.

10. The Larger associations, provide local, national and international prominent guest speakers that are involved in every aspect of real investing, as well *as constantly informing their members of seminars, boot-camps, classes mentoring programs etc.,* that provide them with learning opportunities.
(Source: *Atlanta Foreclosure Report*)

Finding the Owner

How do you find and contact owners of vacant properties? You could drive through the neighborhood and asked the neighbors if they know how to get in touch with the owner. Give them your phone number, and get theirs. Perhaps you can offer them a referral fee. You'd be surprised at what may turn up. Follow-up once a week and ask if they've talked to the owner, or to a daughter, grandson, or anyone that can put you in touch with them. Also, here are three additional methods you can employ:

Method 1   Send a letter or postcard to the address. If it gets forwarded, you can then send a certified letter to the owner. You can say anything you want in the letter, but this information should also be included. "I noticed your property is vacant and I'm interested in buying properties in your area. Do you want to sell your property? Here is my telephone number."

Method 2   Go down to your county courthouse and find out where the most recent tax bill has been sent; then send a letter to that address. Sometimes it will be the address of an attorney's office, or of a third party, but these people usually know where the owner is, and how to contact them.

In addition, this would be a good time to *determine the value* on the property so that you can make a decision whether or not to continue the search. The owner and the property are separate entities. Since property sales and tax information are public record, you can find the value on a property.

You will also need to check for the following information:

▼ **Most recent deed of record.** Find the most recent instrument that secures the deed (i.e. security deed, trust deed, or deed to secure debt).

▼ **Current property value.** Listed on the deed, there is a formula. You will need to find out what that formula is in your state. With this information, you can determine the current property value, and subtract the original debt amount, to see if there is a big enough difference (based on your criteria) to make it worth your while to invest.

▼ **Outstanding Taxes.** Look for the amount of transfer tax paid. Also, check the tax records to see how many outstanding taxes are owed on the property, and if there are any liens filed against it. You can ask the clerk to help you with finding this information.

Method 3   If the previous two methods don't work, and you were unable to find the owner (probably because the property taxes haven't been paid for many years), you may need to use a company that specializes in finding missing persons. They usually charge somewhere between $50 to $100 to find someone. Depending upon the profit to be gained, it may be well worth the $100 to find the owner.

You can also have a title search done by contacting an attorney or a title company. But, you should probably do this only if you feel confident that you can make a profit. For example, you may be able to purchase a property worth $80,000 for 50 cents on the dollar. It would definitely be worth your while to pursue it.

Think About It!

Success is a formula, or a recipe. The ingredients are: 1) desire, 2) commitment, and 3) repetition (we are all creatures of habit). Stir until you get the results you want. People who ultimately become successful in their Real Estate Investment Business are generally successful in other areas in their lives.

"Nothing in the world can take the place of persistence."
—Emma Chappell

Chapter 2
Four Easy Ways to Make Big Profits In Real Estate

It's a Simple Formula

Simply put, making money by investing in real estate has to be done by the numbers. You have to determine what numbers you are willing to work with. Most importantly, you have to look at each deal and decide, based on the numbers, what it is that you want to do with the property **BEFORE** you buy. If you want to sell it, make sure that there's somebody out there who would buy the property.

Step 1: Set up the criteria for your real estate investing program.

Now that you've probably got some idea of how much money you want to make per deal, you can also decide what neighborhoods meet your criteria. This is called your farming area. Here's how.

▼ Look for houses that are in the income range for your area; say approximately $50,000 to $75,000. (This figure may have to be adjusted up or down depending upon where you are located.)

▼ Be able to drive up to 30-minutes away from your home. Your farming area should be within that range.

▼ Be able to make a minimum of $3,000, and an average of $5,000 to $10,000 per deal.

▼ Be able to make a minimum of two deals per year to start. (Depending on your time, you may want to make two deals per month.)

▼ Once a week, be able to make phone calls and visits to build up your team (Appraiser, Accountant, Mortgage Broker, Realtor, Title Company, Real Estate Attorney, Mentor/ Teacher).

Step 2. Locating properties, or more accurately, locating motivated sellers

As a beginner, locate properties of motivated sellers in the following four ways:

1. **Peruse your farming area.**

   Write down information from any signs that say, "For Sale by Owner" (FSBO) or Realtor signs. Be sure to write down the address of the property, and the name of the Realtor who is selling the property, plus any other information posted on the sign. In the case of vacant houses, write down the street address, and if you can, take a picture of the property. Make a folder for each property, and include the picture.

2. **Attend local real estate association meetings.**

   Get flyers from other investors. Oftentimes, you may find a good deal. Sometimes, investors can even assist you with financing information, as well as put you in touch with other resources, such as contractors, attorneys, etc.

3. **Hook up with a good realtor that works with investors.**

   You will find them at your association meetings you can also find them in the newspapers, through referrals and some-times just by calling the office. If you see realtor signs that say foreclosure, contact that office. Oftentimes, these realtors will work with investors.

FYI: Acquiring Vacant Properties

If a property has been sitting for years, you may be able to contact the owner and get a signed contract. The property may need a lot of work before it is livable.

If you're not able to fix the property yourself, an option would be to sell or ASSIGN the contract to another investor, with more experience, who can do the work. He/she will later profit from the deal, but the money you gained is better than nothing.

Another option might be to find a partner; perhaps a general contractor experienced in rehabs. You could work with them and split the profits.

4. **Last but not least, search newspaper ads.**

Both major, and local throw a-ways have FSBO (For Sale by Owner) ads. Call everyone.

Step 3. Real Estate By the Numbers

If used correctly, the following three forms can make you rich. (Also, see "Forms" in Chapter 5)

Form 1—Seller Information Script

The questions in this form are pretty self-explanatory. It's all in the delivery. You must ask questions with confidence and with care. Motivated sellers will usually answer all of the questions that they can.

Listen for two pieces of information:

1) How much they say the property is worth.

2) How much they owe on the property (including loans, liens, and arrears).

If you wish to proceed, you would then set up an appointment to meet the seller, and request that they bring with them the following list of items:

- ▼ All deeds, notes (first, second, third mortgages)
- ▼ Last payment to lender
- ▼ Last paid tax bill
- ▼ Last paid insurance bill
- ▼ Documentation on any liens
- ▼ Mandatory association dues or fees

If it turns out that the property is in foreclosure, or the seller has filed bankruptcy, the property can still be purchased. Contact your local real estate association for information/laws on how purchase foreclosed or bankrupt properties in your area.

Form 2—Property Evaluation Profile

After your appointment, use the information the seller provided to fill out your Property Evaluation Profile form. This form allows you to "run your numbers" to determine if this investment would be profitable.

Form 3—Property Repair Analysis

This form is also self-explanatory. When you meet the seller at the property, walk around the house, inside and out, making note of everything you see wrong, in every room, as well as on the exterior of the house. Use your repair sheet as a guideline. After you leave the property, you can determine the cost of repairs.

Here's An Idea!

A good idea would be to have someone familiar with repairs accompany you as you look through the property with the seller, even if it's just a handyman. Or, you can set up an appointment with the handyman at a later time, to give the property a more thorough check.

Step 4. Submitting Your First Offer
Due Diligence & The Property Acquisition Sheet

You learned above about using three forms (Seller Information Call Sheet, Property Inspection Summary, and Estimating Property Repair Analysis) that will make you rich. Take a moment to look them up in Chapter Five. Then, estimate as soon as you can what the costs will be to buy the property; profit from the property; repair the property; and hold the property, until you can sell it. Without that information, you really can't make a good decision.

However, there will be times when moving quickly to determine profitability can mean the difference between keeping, or losing a good deal. Your *Acquisition Sheet* (form) will allow you to see your overall costs, line-by-line. Fill in every blank, and when you're done, you'll have the number that will tell you if the property is something worth pursuing.

Overcoming Your Fear

Many African Americans fear taking the first investment step for reasons ranging from thinking they don't have enough knowledge, money, skill, connections, etc. From now on, you must decide that you are on the wealth track. You must "Assume the Position" and act as if you are already where you want to be.

Investor's Fear

In the Real Estate Investment Business, you must be able to make decisions in a timely fashion. The fear of putting your signature on the dotted line stems from wondering what you are going to lose if you invest.

The worst possible thing that can happen (because most real estate contracts have a liquidation clause) is that you lose your dollar earnest money deposit. So, make sure you use money that you can afford to lose.

To some African Americans, even the smallest loss could be devastating. If losing your earnest money deposit means that you are going to lose your house, or can't eat, etc., you probably shouldn't invest at this time.

Just a Precaution!

If you find yourself in a deal that you don't think is good, walk away! Write it off as a loss (which you can do at the end of the tax year), and go on to the next prospect. It happens to the best of real estate investors at some point in time.

An ideal amount of investment money to have in reserve would be $5,000 to $10,000. This will cover the earnest money deposit, closing costs, and possible up front repair costs.

Part 3—Making the Offer

Once you've completed the three preliminary forms, and had your contractor give you the "okay" on the property, it's time to make the offer. If you are afraid to take this first step alone, then ask someone to go with you—a friend, a fellow investor, a family member, a mentor and/or a teacher—but, **MAKE THE OFFER!**

Put this clause in you special stipulations section: "The earnest money deposit check is to be deposited within 24 hours after all the contingencies have been removed from the contract." This clause will allow you 3-14 days to verify information without risking any money.

Will all seller's accept this clause? No. Those that are motivated will; those that aren't won't. So what! NEXT!! (Remember do not spend your time on unmotivated sellers.)

In time, because you will have done your homework, and you'll know when it's a good deal, you will make offers as an experienced investor. And you'll realize that, like most good deals, it will not stay on the market very long.

Think about it!

If you don't remember anything else from this guide, remember this (circle it, highlight it, underline it): *You never just look for properties, you look for situations.*

"Set your goals high and don't stop until you get there!"
—Bo Jackson

Chapter 3
Financing Your Real Estate Investment Business

One of the biggest myths in Real Estate Investing is that you've got to have a lot of cash to start. If the deal is good enough, someone will fund it.

"Can you buy property No Money Down (NMD)? is a frequently asked question. Yes, you can, but what the question really means to ask is, "Can you buy property with *NO DOWN PAYMENT?*" The answer is a definite YES!

However, can you close a real estate transaction without any money? No, or very seldom. There are always certain costs associated with closing a real estate transaction. They're called "closing costs". They typically run approximately 1 to 3 percent of the total amount of the loan.

These costs include but are not limited to the following :
- ▼ Payment to the lender for administrative costs (Origination Fee or Points)
- ▼ Payment to the mortgage broker for commission
- ▼ Payment to the closing attorney or the title company for closing the loan
- ▼ Costs for the pro-rated taxes and insurance (pre-paids)
- ▼ Payment to the county clerk's office for the transferring of documents

▼ Costs to pay Realtors commissions

▼ Miscellaneous, other costs for appraisals, surveys, title searches, etc.

Again, closing costs generally range from one to three percent of the total loan (1 point = 1 percent). For example, if the total loan amount is $100,000 and the lender charges 3 points to originate the loan, the charge would be $3,000 or 3 %. If the other closing costs are another $3,000 then the total closing costs would be $6,000 which is not uncommon for an investor loan of that amount. So, you could purchase the property for no money down, but someone would still have to produce approximately $6,000 for closing costs.

FYI: The 411 about Closing Costs

Certain states require that both the seller and the buyer pay certain closing costs. Also, contracts that realtors prepare always state the amount of closing costs the seller will pay. This can be open to negotiation, but you should look for that clause before you sign a contract with a Realtor.

Before we proceed, let's define two types of terms we should use:

Term 1—Loan To Value (LTV)

This is the amount a lender is willing to loan against the value of the property. For example, if a property is appraised at a value of $100,000 a lender may be willing to lend 80 percent LTV or $80,000.

You may be aware of situations where people borrow 125% LTV, meaning that they actually borrow 25% more than the property is worth. Usually, those loans are funded by private investment lenders and the rules for those loans are regulated differently.

Term 2—After Repair Value (ARV)

When property is purchased "as is", this means that you are purchasing it in its current unrepaired state. Of course, you'll get it at a much better price when the property is repaired. However, the lender wants to know beforehand, what it will be worth, after the repairs are made (ARV). An appraiser will be used to perform what is called a "subject to appraisal".

This means that the property will be appraised, pursuant to the needed repairs. The cost to repair the property becomes part of the appraisal value. For example, if you purchase an investment property for $40,000 and your list of repairs costs $20,000 the property will be appraised at $60,000. Once you have completed the repairs, the value of the property would then be $100,000 (based upon, for example, what similar properties in the neighborhood are worth). So the actual value of the property, with repairs, is $100,000.

The Importance of Insurance When Doing Your Deals

Whenever you purchase a piece of property it must be insured in order to protect the investment for both you and the lender .The type of insurance needed depends on the state of the property.

There are several types of insurance that may be placed on a property. When you get ready to close on a property however the lender will generally require the following kinds of insurance.

Note: The specific terms and conditions are unique to each policy

▼ Type I—Lender's Insurance Requirements for Closings.

a) "**Hazard Insurance**" is called "Homeowners Insurance" if you live in the property, and it's called "Renter Dwelling Insurance" if it's and investment property".

The primary purpose of "Hazard Insurance" is to cover the dwelling and to provide for the replacement costs of the improvement (house) in the event it should be totally destroyed… such as from a fire.

Note: If you let this insurance lapse for any reason, the lender will provide a policy and charge you for it. It will be added to your mortgage payment, generally at a much higher cost than you could find on the open market.

b) The other insurance generally required by the lender, at closing, is called "**Lender's Title Insurance**" This insurance protects the lender against any defect in the title.

If you also want to be covered under this insurance you must purchase "**Owners Title Insurance.**" This insurance will cover you if the title company overlooked some problem with the chain of title; and, if a lawsuit arises due to that oversight, you can then sue them for not doing their job.

Note: I highly recommend you purchase "Owner's Title insurance" it might be the best money you ever spent.

▼ **Type 2—Insurance Necessary for New Construction Rehabilitation and Restorations**

"**Builders Risk Insurance**"—this type of insurance covers property while it's being built, rehabilitated or restored. The primary purpose of this insurance is to cover the building, building materials, and equipment necessary during the building phase. This insurance is usually more expensive compared to regular hazard insurance, and is very specific about what it covers. "Builders Risk Insurance" is usually short-term, for less than 6 months. There are very few companies that issue this type of insurance.

▼ **Type 3—Mortgage Insurance (MI) or Private Mortgage Insurance (PMI)**

Lenders use formulas to determine whether to place "**PMI or MI**" on a loan.

One formula that many government insurers, such as Housing and Urban Development (HUD) or Veterans Administration (VA) use is based on Loan to Value (LTV).

The magic number with many government lenders is 80% loan to value. This means that if you purchase a home worth $100,000 the government will lend you up to $80,000 or 80% LTV without charging mortgage insurance. In essence, the lender is saying they will keep $20,000 equity or 20% LTV in the property.

Basically, it's their cushion in case something should go wrong. If you say, for instance, that you want to borrow $85,000 or 85% LTV on your $100,000 they would probably say: "OK, but to guarantee our loan we will charge you **"Mortgage Insurance"**. This will assure that we (the lender) get paid in case something goes wrong."

Types of Financing

There are four common categories of financing available to you as a real estate investor:

1. Hard Money loans.
2. Joint Partnership loans
3. Seller financing
4. Conventional loans

Hard Money Lenders.

Hard Money Lenders are often large companies located all over the United States. But in some cases, they are single individuals.

Typically, clients of hard money lenders are private individuals who have funds to lend, and who are looking for high returns on their investment. Hard money lenders always look at the property, not the borrower. Generally, the requirements for the borrower are as follows:

a. An application from the borrower (this is just a formality).

b. A credit report from the borrower (You don't need good credit, but it could affect the points you are charged, and the interest rate you receive.)

Hard money loans are generally made under the following terms:

a. The Lenders usually hire their own appraisers. The loan is always subject to appraisal.

b. You would be required to use licensed contractors from your local area for repairs.

c. They are usually short-term loans, two years or less, but amortized over thirty years.

You are generally charged points anywhere from four to ten percent (remember, one point = 1% of the loan amount). You are also generally charged an interest rate anywhere from four to eighteen percent, depending upon the real estate market.

d. Hard money loans are generally interest only loans. That is, during the term of the loan you never pay anything toward the principal amount, so at the end of the loan you will still owe full amount of principal.

e. When you pay this loan, there's usually what is called a "prepayment penalty" attached. This could be a percentage of the interest. For example, a prepayment penalty of three months interest, or a flat amount may be charged.

You can always be assured of making some money using hard money lenders. Sometimes, if you have as little as $1,000 in closing costs, the hard money lenders may even roll those closing costs into the loan. For example, say you purchased a property for $40,000. A hard money lender will pay that $40,000, plus give you $20,000 for repairs (*Note: The funds for repairs are given in increments, as each phase of the work is completed*).

After repairs, the property is now worth $100,000. You would then sell it, pay off your $60,000 debt to the hard money lender, and make approximately $40,000. You will have highly leveraged your money. This is comparable to a "No Money Down" deal.

However, there can also be tax disadvantages to using Hard Money Lenders. There can be extremely high tax consequences if you use hard money to purchase properties, then re-sell or "flip them".

Take Note:

If the loan came from a Hard Money Lender, and the property was "flipped", the net profit could be substantially less. For example, if the federal tax rate for the seller is 26 percent, and his state tax rate is seven percent, and his social security tax rate is 15 percent; a grand total of 48 percent, this would mean $.48 cents of out of every dollar would go to taxes. Therefore, you would actually clear $23,360 out of a potential $40,000 profit.

Remember, the types of real estate investment situations we are generally looking for, are those where the value is already there, or where value can be created by doing repairs. Here's a "buy low-sell high" example:

Let's say an elderly person has owned the property for 30 years. The value of the property has appreciated greatly. This three-bedroom, one-bath house was originally purchased for $14,700. There is a current pay off of $3,500 and the property is in foreclosure. It would take about $12,000 worth of repairs to bring the house back to good condition. The appraised value of the house today is $100,000. The owner wants $40,000 which is more than double his investment. The deal looks like this:

> $100,000 Appraised Value
> -$40,000 Payoff to Owner
> **$60,000 Sub-total**
> $12,000 Necessary Repairs
> **$48,000 Gross Profit to Buyer**
> -$5,000 Financing and Holding Cost
> = **$43,000 NET PROFIT!**

This is a win-win-win-win-win situation. 1) The owner wins, 2) the investor wins, 3) the contractor that made the referral wins 4) the buyer wins, 5) and, the neighbors win.

Joint Venture Partnership funding

This type of loan assumes that you want a partner to finance a deal that you've located. This deal would be based strictly on what you negotiate with a partner. You would draw up some type of agreement; usually a joint venture agreement, that would include (but not be limited to):

1. The parties or entities to the transaction or agreement.

2. The terms of the transaction; who will provide the funds and for how long; how the assets and liabilities will be divided; and how will ownership and equity be divided. The agreement should also include a termination clause; in other words, how can the partnership be dissolved if by mutual agreement.

Seller Financing

There are two methods of seller financing:
> 1) Wrap-around Mortgage
> 2) Lease Options

You should contact a closing attorney, or a title company to have these documents written up. On the top of every wraparound note it should say wraparound mortgage. You and the seller may also be required to sign a statement saying you understand that the lender may call the loan if there is a "due on sales clause" in the original loan that you are taking subject to. This type of closing should cost $200 or less.

1. **Wrap-around Mortgage**

A Wrap-around Mortgage is when a buyer purchases a property "subject to the existing loan". For example, you're going to purchase a property from the seller for $75,000. The seller already has secured funds from ABC lender, with a balance of $40,000, a six percent interest rate, and 15 years remaining on the loan. You agree to take the property over with the $40,000 loan—$322.15 per month, including: principal interest, taxes, and insurance (PITI). There will also be a new loan created for the remaining

$35,000 ($40,000 plus $35,000 equals the $75,000) you agreed to pay the seller. The $35,000 loan will be paid as follows:

The loan would be amortized over thirty years with an interest rate of 10 percent. The payment on the new loan would be $307.15 per month. The new loan is called a " wraparound loan". This loan can be created without any up front money to the seller; just by the buyer agreeing to pay $629.30 per month for the next 15 years, until the underlying loan is paid off. The new loan would adjust down for the last 15 years. Comparably, this too, could be considered a NO MONEY DOWN deal.

Just A Precaution!

Three things to do with this type of seller's financing:

1. Purchase title insurance on the property.

2. Set up an escrow account whereby you can make your payments each month. Then have a third party pay the note, complete and send you documentation of payments on a monthly, quarterly, or semi-annual basis, whenever you choose.

3. Add your name on to the insurance policy as an additional insured, in case something happens, and the insurance company has to pay out a claim.

2. **Lease Options**

The best types of property for lease options are properties that are in excellent condition, need little or no repairs, have little or no equity. In addition, the seller would need primarily debt relief, rather than cash up front. There are many situations and/or circumstances where the seller may be willing to sell the property as a lease option. A Lease Option (L/O) is when someone agrees to purchase a property at a future date, under agreed-upon terms.

Lease options are probably the most negotiable deals of all. The buyer would agree to buy the seller's house within the next three years or the seller can take it back.

As the buyer, you might agree to the following:

1. Make the payments for the next three years. Exercise your option to buy the property under the agreed upon terms within the three years.

2. Keep the property maintained.

3. Allow the seller to continue to write off the taxes and interest. (This is a negotiable point)

It is very important that you negotiate with the seller for him/her to pay one or two of the payments before you sign your L/O agreement. This gives you time to find a buyer for your option agreement. You as a person holding the option can sell the property. This is yet another comparable "NO MONEY DOWN" deal.

For example, a seller's job is moving him/her to another state within the next 60 days. If the seller cannot sell the house he/she is currently living in, they may agree to sell the house to you on a L/O.

Turns out, the property is in very good condition and is valued at $120,000. The balance owed on the property is $90,000 at a seven and one half percent interest rate. The current payment is $598, which covers the principal and interest. The taxes and insurance are another $150 per month. Therefore, the current payment is $750 per month.

If the property is in a neighborhood that rents for $950 to $1000 per month, and the owner agrees to sell you the property for $105,000 on a three year option, you can make money three different ways:

a. You can sell the property on a lease option to someone else for more than what you are paying. For example, if you are purchasing the property for $105,000, you can sell it for a two and one half year option for $125,000, making a $20,000 profit.

(Note: you want their option agreement to end before your option agreement does with the seller).

b.   You would charge the new buyers an option fee to be applied to their down payment at the time of purchase. This could be anywhere from two to five percent of the purchase price.

Option Amount Paid to Investor from the Optionee (two and one half percent of $125,000 = $3,125)

c.   You can split between what you have to pay for the monthly note and what you charge your purchasers. If you pay $750 each month, you can charge a new purchaser $950 to $1,000 per month, if this price is comparable to neighborhood rental fees.

In some cases, the lease option purchaser is willing to pay a little extra each month towards their future down payment. These tenants may want to pay $1,100 per month and have $100 per month go toward their down payment.

Optionee pays $1,100 per month. Investor pays $750 towards principle plus interest taxes and insurance. $1100- $750 = $350@ month. Therefore, the difference between the split is $350 times 34 months, which equals $11,900.

Total Amount made on this L/O transaction is: **$35,025.**

FYI...the 411 About L/O

L/Os don't require that you close until you exercise the option in three years. You should, however, do the following three things.

1. Record the option agreement in the county courthouse

2. Set up an escrow account for the payments, which include an accounting mechanism.

3. Have your name added on the insurance policy as an additional insured.

Conventional Financing

Loans such as VA, FHA, Fannie Mae and Freddie Mac, are typically secured by the United States Government and therefore are considered safer loans for lenders. However, these types of loans are usually more difficult to secure.

Conventional lenders now have specific programs for investors. These programs, however, require the borrower to provide full documentation, in order to acquire the loan. Here is a list of general requirements:

▼ A good credit score.
▼ A five to thirty percent down payment
▼ A reserve of three to six months worth of loan payments
▼ Tax records for the previous two years.
▼ If you're operating as a business, proof of income for a minimum of three years.
▼ An appraisal (usually conducted by one of their own appraisers, or one they approve).

This loan is typically taken out by people wanting to buy a home to live in. If there is a less than 80 percent loan-to-value, you will pay private mortgage insurance (PMI). Once the loan-to-value reaches 80 percent or more, you can then request to have the PMI removed. After a year of owning the property, if you haven't been late on any of the mortgage payments, you could easily refinance, get a better interest rate with better terms, and in some cases, you can get some cash back, too.

There are also lenders that will allow you to refinance immediately after you take ownership. It's called a loan that requires no seasoning. Typically though, you will pay higher interest rates on these types of loans.

Think About It!

The safer the loan, the lower the interest rate; the lower the interest rate, the lower the payment; the lower the payment, the higher the cash flow.

"It doesn't matter how many say it cannot be done or how many people have tried it before; it's important to realize that whatever you're doing, it's your first attempt at it."
—Wally Amos

Chapter 4
Know When To Sell or Hold Your Property...

In reality, your Real Estate Investment Business, will offer you only two options: To sell, or to hold. However, from these two options, you need to ask yourself "how" you want to invest. Here are the various options or plans to consider in your real estate investment initiative.

What is your plan?

1. Purchase and resell without rehabbing
2. Purchase and resell with rehabbing
3. Purchase and resell without owning
4. Purchase, rehab, refinance, and hold
5. Purchase and hold with cosmetic fix-ups
6. Purchase, hold and rent

Using the options above, you can decide how you will use your real estate investment property. These are some narrowed-down options.

You can "Purchase and Resell" a property in a number of ways: wholesale, retail, lease option, seller financed, or contract assignment.

However, there are two primary ways to Purchase and Hold property:

▼ **Purchase, hold, and use the property as your primary residence**

That is, purchase a property with the intent of using it as your permanent residence. There are favorable tax laws, in some states, for your permanent residence. For example, if you *live* in a property for any two of five years, you can sell it for up to $250,000 if you are single, and up to $500,000, if you are married, and not have to pay capital gains (check with your accountant for complete information concerning this law).

FYI—Benefits of Purchase, Hold and Rent

The following are the positive aspects of renting property to tenants:

a. Provides a monthly income
b. Allows for appreciation
c. Provides for equity build-up
d. Permits you to leverage your time and money

▼ **Purchase, hold, and rent the property to tenants for income**

Rental property is one of the most lucrative long-term investments in real estate; and if this is the option you choose, it must be viewed as a "business". The biggest challenge with owning rental properties is choosing the right TENANTS. Now that you are ready to join the ranks of rental property investors, here are some simple steps in securing good tenants:

Advertise

Advertise in places that your perfect tenant might be found. For example, put fliers on bulletin boards at companies where people work. Put ads in your local newspaper with the largest circulation; usually the paid newspapers, not the throw a-ways. Ask your Real Estate Broker, or other members of your "Dream Team".

Screen Your Applicants

Many African-American real estate investors have told horror stories about renters. In almost every case, they failed to screen them properly. The following procedures can be used to screen tenants.

Screening #1:

Place a Simple Ad in the Newspaper. Create a telephone script. The message should give a potential tenant specific instructions. For example, "If you're calling regarding the one bedroom house, push one." If they are interested in setting up an appointment, ask them to leave their name, a day and evening telephone number, and state, "we will return your call within 24 hours." People that do not follow these simple instructions should not rent your property.

Screening #2:

The Potential Tenant Called You with his name and phone number, wishing to set up an appointment. Always keep your word by returning calls within 24 hours, as promised. Set up a convenient appointment time, and inform potential tenants that they will be required to fill out an application, plus bring any application fee charges.

Also, you can require them to bring information such as references, checks stubs, and to complete necessary paperwork. If they have children, ask them to bring them to the appointment, too. If the children are bouncing off the walls during the appointment, and the potential tenant isn't responding favorably to the behavior, this a true sign of the way they're going to treat your property.

Screening #3:

Require the Potential Tenant to Call you one hour prior to your appointment to confirm. If they fail to confirm, don't go to the appointment.

Screening #4:

Are the Tenants on Time? Observe everything. How are they dressed? How are they interacting with their children? Did they bring what you asked?

Screening #5:

The Application. Have them complete the application. After it is completed, review the application, and any other necessary forms (i.e. verification of employment form, landlord request form, etc.) Make sure they complete the previous and current landlord reference section. In addition, require them to provide at least two references from **close** relatives, including their telephone numbers and addresses. In the event that you need to contact the tenant, the best way to do so is through one of these relatives.

Screening # 6:

The Application Fee (usually $20 to $35). This fee should be separate from any other monies you will collect from the potential tenant. You can require that under no circumstances will this fee be returned (use your own discretion). Explain to the applicant that it will take at least three business days to verify their information.

Call the potential tenant's current and former landlord (unless it's a relative). The information gained, should be used as a major deciding factor to rent to this person. You can use a renter's service to pull the potential tenant's credit. These services can also check for evictions, employment, and criminal backgrounds. Always verify employment. You can do this by contacting the personnel or human resources department where the potential tenant works.

Screening #7:

Rental Reservation Form. After choosing a potential tenant, you should require a deposit; for example $200 (out of $600). Use a Rental Reservation Form. Complete this form and give a copy to the tenant. This form explains what the deposit is for, and how it can be used, etc. Give the potential tenant a receipt. Did the candidate give you the $400 balance of the deposit when it was due?

We have discussed seven screening points that are very important. After interviewing and screening two to three candidates, you should be able to make an objective decision from collectively reviewing their information, and choosing from the strongest candidate. Tell the candidates to check back with you in a few days. By then you will be able to let the unsuccessful candidates know that they did not get the property, so they can continue their search for a residence, and you can move forward with the candidate that you chose.

Just a Precaution:

Most employers perform criminal background checks before they hire employees; so you would want the same peace of mind when it comes to renting your property to a stranger. The good news is, as a prerequisite for Section 8 housing, applicants have already had a criminal background check. So, after all is said and done, you should just go with your gut.

Section 8

Another good way to find tenants and have a guaranteed rental income is by offering Section 8 Housing. Section 8 is funded by The Housing and Urban Development Office of the government (also known as HUD). Recent legislation has changed Section 8 to only allow people to be on the program for a limited time. Women in the program are now required to work at least part-time, and participate in their own financial future.

If you are willing to list your property on Section 8, you would then need to advertise on their property listings.

The procedure for becoming a Section 8 Landlord varies from state to state. However, in most cases, Section 8 vouchers are portable, meaning they can be transferred from one state or city, to another. In order to become a Section 8 Landlord, you must personally go to the appropriate Section 8 office (in some states, you can apply online). You will then get a "briefing" on their particular rules and regulations. Once your paperwork has been submitted, Section 8 authorizes a "call/view", and sets up an appointment to inspect your property.

The day your property passes inspection, Section 8 authorizes a contract stating that you are now a Section 8 Landlord. As a Section 8 Landlord, you are required to maintain your property according to Section 8 criteria, which includes providing safe and clean housing for your tenants.

When your Section 8 tenant moves in, you get paid the negotiated monthly rent, on the first day of each month, until the contract expires (generally in one year). This is **guaranteed** income, as long as you perform under the contract. Like any other government program, Section 8 is revised almost annually. Therefore, it is important that you keep track for updates. As a rule, Section 8 performs an annual inspection and authorizes a new, sure contract each year.

Below is an example of how Section 8 can be used in relation to the business of rental property.

Example. You are currently paying approximately $1,171 per month for a three-bedroom, one-bathroom house. Subtracting utilities, your monthly payment would be $970. If you decide to use Section 8, as a rule, the rental payments should cover your mortgage payment. Conservatively, five units netting $150 per month each, would give you an income of $750 per month. Multiply that times twelve, and you will have earned $9,000 over one year. Using Section 8, you could make a substantial income, particularly if you begin to invest in duplex, quads and multi-units.

Special Housing at a Glance
Inspections: Rent Ready Criteria

The following criteria is provided as a *generalized checklist* used in determining a rent ready unit for Section 8 participants and serves as a guide in preparing for the inspection. Other items not listed below may cause the unit to fail. **All county, city and state codes must be followed.**

1. All utilities on and operating safely.

2. Roof, gutter, facia boards, foundation and exterior walls structurally sound and weather tight.

3. Windows and exterior doors function properly, weather tight, and lockable.

4. Window screens installed on all windows, if unit does not have a properly working A/C.

5. Bathroom doors must lock. Bedroom doors are not required to lock.

6. Stairs, porches and rails must be structurally sound.

7. Handrails for stairs, and guardrails for porches, if required. Generally 4 or more steps for stairs require handrails, and porches 30 inches above ground require guardrails.

8. Properly installed smoke detector on each level of dwelling unit.

9. Adequate heat to all rooms used for living.

10. Water heater properly installed and operable.

11. All plumbing properly installed, leak free and properly vented as required.

12. Approved refuge disposal provided.

13. Site and interior of house free of garbage, debris and infestation.

14. Unit must be vacant and free of any landlord possessions (No storage of any kind including automobiles, furniture, etc.).

15. Stove and refrigerator must function properly and safely.

16. All interior walls, floors and ceilings are safe, structurally sound and weather tight.

17. All painted surfaces free from peeling, chipping, scaling and loose paint.

18. Safe and sanitary conditions throughout.

19. Provide adequate and properly functioning electrical outlets, switches and fixtures.

20. All rooms of unit must be accessible and bedroom ceiling must be at least 7ft.

Completing The Lease Agreement

The lease agreement is probably the most important document that you will need, when it comes to rental property. This is a document that you would take to court. The information therein contains the clauses you must use, especially when you evict a tenant. You must use this procedure, in order to successfully evict a tenant, legally.

Generally, you would contact the tenant about a lease violation, in writing, and in the form of a warning. There are many reasons for evicting a tenant, in addition to non-payment of rent. These reasons should be found in the lease agreement. However, there are some lease violations that do not require a previous warning. For example, violating county, state, or federal law, such as drug trafficking would not require a warning for eviction.

Below are some important points to consider when setting up your lease agreement. Your lease agreement should include:

1) An automatic increase (note this cannot be used with Section 8 tenants) at renewal.

2) After the one-year term has expired, the lease automatically becomes a month-to-month occupancy.

3) The names and numbers of people who are eligible to live in the property for more than fourteen days.

4) Additional clauses. For example, a clause that says the tenant is responsible for the first $50 for repairs, per occurrence.

This letter and form for new, renewing and late tenants is recommended by *Home Rental Publishing*.

Dear Tenant:

You rent is due on the __ day of the month. I'm sure you fully understand that we must start eviction proceedings Immediately, once a payment Is late (no matter the reason) and report your late payment to both local and national tenant/credit reporting agencies. We still request however, that you submit your reason for late payment for our records. For your convenience, and to avoid lengthy explanation, you may simply check the appropriate reason below and submit this form with your late payment. Hopefully this form and your payment will be received before you're evicted. Even better, your payments will arrive on-time and you will not need this form.

I'm Sorry My Rent Is Late But...

☐ A. The check I've been waiting for did not come in the mail or was late.

☐ B. I was in the hospital/jail and I couldn't get to you.

☐ C. I missed a week's work because I had to take care of my sick mother/son/daughter.

☐ D. I had to have some teeth pulled and the dentist won't start work until I give him some money.

☐ E. I was in an automobile accident and I won't have any money until my attorney works things out with the other guy's insurance.

☐ F. I had my billfold stolen when this guy jumped me on my way to the bank/post-office/your office.

☐ G. Someone broke into my apartment and took my money. No, I didn't file a police report...Should I?

☐ H. I had to have my car fixed so I could get to work, so I could pay you.

☐ I. My mother/sister/uncle hasn't mailed me my money yet.

❑ J. I couldn't find your address. I put the wrong address on the envelope.

❑ K. I got laid off from my job and I won't get unemployment for a couple of weeks.

❑ L. I was not able to get a money order and I know you didn't want me to send cash.

❑ M. You didn't come by when I had the money.

❑ N. My husband/wife/boyfriend/girlfriend/roommate left and I didn't have all the money.

❑ O. They garnished my check and I don't understand it, because the guy told me it would be okay to just pay so much per month and I only missed a couple of payments.

❑ P. I told my friend to bring it or send it to you while I was out of town.

❑ O. I haven't received my tax refund yet.

❑ R. I got a new job, and I had to work three weeks before I got my first check.

❑ S. I didn't pay the rent because my _____is not fixed. No, I'm sorry I didn't tell you there was a problem before now. I didn't think about it until now.

❑ T. My car is broken and I didn't have a ride to your office/the post office.

❑ U. I had to help my brother/sister/friend who had a serious problem.

❑ V. My grandmother died and I had to go to the funeral.

❑ W. I didn't have, or I forgot to put, a stamp on the envelope.

❑ X. The check's in the mail. Didn't you get it?

❑ Y . I ran out of checks.

❑ Z. I'm dead!

Please briefly explain if your excuse is not listed above:

_____

_____

Now you've done all the preliminary work and you feel really good about your decision. But, before you sign on the dotted line, know that you have evaluated and weighed all your options. Ask yourself if you would be able to evict a woman and her three children? Or any tenant, for that matter, who you became attached to? What would your answer be? Yes? No? Here's the situation: The mortgage must be paid every month. Either your tenant pays your mortgage, or you pay...case closed.

If you cannot evict tenants, you will end up paying your own mortgage, while taking care of the tenant, and his or her children. If this is not an ideal situation, then you must evict this tenant, in order to allow another tenant to come in and pay your mortgage.

So, if your answer is no—to evicting tenants—then you do not need to be in the rental property investment business. However, a remedy to this could be to hire a rental management company to do the eviction. But, also understand that no one will take care of your property as well as you; and, if you do decide to hire a rental management company, you now may have double the work...to watch both the management company, and your tenant.

Meeting With the Tenant To Sign the Lease

The final step is meeting with the tenant and going over the lease. At this meeting, you will point out any important points, that you deem necessary, and make sure the tenant understands everything within the lease. You will collect any additional monies owed. You will give receipts, and an inspection check.

Think About It!

Renting property is a business, and must be administered as such. Make sure your tenant is someone who will take care of your property. Renting to friends and family members may be ideal, but it could backfire in the long run...feelings can be hurt, and friendships ruined. Make sure you cover all bases before you make any Purchase, Hold and Rent Real Estate Investment Decisions.

The main reason I wanted to be successful
was to get out of the ghetto.
—Florence Griffith-Joyner

Chapter 5

Basic Real Estate Forms that Can Save You Thousands of Dollars

Forms play an essential part of the success of your Real Estate Investment Business. Well-developed forms can save you literally thousands of dollars, and in many cases actually make you money.

In this chapter, we list and discuss in detail the basic forms needed to get you started in your real estate investment business. (Although, I have listed the primary forms, they are, by no means, all-inclusive.)

Forms Used to Find...Fund and Farm Your Real Estate Property

Category 1: Forms Used for Finding and Evaluating Properties

▼ **Seller information form**—used to collect information on the seller, the property and most of all the circumstances of the deal

▼ **Cash flow form**—determines if there will be money left over each month after all expenses are paid

▼ **Property rehabilitation checklist form**—(Quick Check Inspection List)—determines what repairs are necessary

▼ **Property rehabilitation cost estimation form**—(Estimating Rehabilitation Cost Using Contractors)—identifies the cost connected to each repair

▼ **Property acquisition costs**

Category 2: Forms Used for the Purchasing/Sale of Property
Note: The forms in this section can be used for both buying and selling

▼ **Real estate purchase and sales agreement**—submitted to seller by the buyer describing the price terms and conditions of the sale of a piece of property

▼ **Addendum to real estate purchase and sales agreement**—used to make changes to the original offer (not included)

▼ **Offer of intent to purchase real estate**—Letter given to the seller describing general terms of the buyer's offer not generally binding, but gets a dialogue started

▼ **Lease with option to purchase real estate agreement**—Offer to purchase property at a specified later date under specified terms and conditions, an option binds the seller but not the buyer. (not included)

▼ **Affidavit and memorandum of agreement concerning real estate**—(Assignment of purchase and sales agreement rights)—gives the rights of a sales contract to another person, usually for a fee.

▼ **Affidavit and memorandum of agreement**—document that is filed at the county courthouse showing that there is a current accepted offer on the property. This clouds the title to the property thus preventing them from changing their mind and selling to someone else.

▼ **Deeds (warranty, quitclaim)** there are several different types of deeds—all used to transfer title from one person or entity to another.

▼ **Closing statement**—instructions from the lender issued to the closing attorney, escrow or title company telling them what documents to be signed, the disbursement of funds and how title is to be transferred.

▼ **Bill of sale**—used to transfer title of personal property. For example, appliances that are a part of a real estate property sale could require the use of a separate bill of sale.

Category 3—Forms Used to Secure Real Estate Debt

▼ **Personal note**—(Deposit Note)—Document that is the evidence of debt used in seller–financing

▼ **Installment note**—evidences debt and describes payment schedule, amount of payment, length of loan and terms of loan including interest rate

▼ **Promissory note**—similar to an IOU allows payment over time can be substituted for a check

▼ **Wrap-around mortgage and security agreement**—A temporary transfer of property to a creditor as a collateral for a loan. **Note:** Each state uses their own form(s) to secure debt on property. The wrap-around mortgage is just one example of a debt instrument.

▼ **Addendum to Wrap-Around Mortgage**—used to make changes to the original mortgage offer. (**not included**)

▼ **Joint Venture agreement**—an agreement between two or more parties delineating an arrangement of how the entities will pay for, purchase and hold a piece of property.

Category 4—Forms Used for Renovations and Repairs for Property (not included)

▼ **Rehab/job estimate sheet**—(Bid Sheet / Checklist)—Contractor completes and submits with his bid estimate. Shows estimated costs and materials list

▼ **Independent contractors agreement**—denotes as an independent contractor delineates the terms and conditions of project also provides contractors personal information

▼ **Amendment to Independent contractors agreement**— used to make changes to the original agreement.

Category 5—Forms Used for Renting, Leasing and/or Evicting Tenants (not included)

▼ **Rental application**—needed information to determine applicants eligibility for renting

▼ **Landlord verification**—used to confirm prior rental obligations.

▼ **Employment verification**—used to confirm applicants work history.

▼ **Month to month rental agreement**—terms on rental based on 30 day termination for either the tenant or the landlord

▼ **Standard residential lease/rental agreement**—most often used for binding renters for 1 year spelling out the terms payment and condition of renting a particular property (see list of excuses that will not be accepted when rent is late)

▼ **Rental reserve deposit form**—agreement that states tenant will pay a specific security deposit in order to reserve the apartment.

▼ **Move-in move out inspection form**—used to determine condition of property at the beginning and end or a rental period, helps to determine if a deposit refund is appropriate and if not why not.

▼ **Notice of overdue rent**—commonly called late fee notice (warning notice) issued the day after rent is due.

▼ **Thirty-day notice to terminate tenancy**—used with month to month rental agreements.

▼ **Notice to pay or quit**—form used to start the eviction procedure in most states.

Although the Purchase and Sales Agreement could be the most important form you will encounter in the business of Real Estate Investing, all other forms listed are vital to your success, as well.

There are several different versions of purchase and sales agreement forms, used in most transactions, when buying or selling a property. Most of those purchase and sales agreements, although in different formats, include four standard elements or parts.

Below is a brief explanation of the parts of a standard **Real Estate Purchase and Sales Agreement**.

Part 1   In almost all real estate purchase and sale agreements, you will fill in the names of the parties to the agreement, the buyer and the seller, then the description of the property in legal and layman's terms (meaning the street address), and the city, county, and state in which it is located.

Part 2   This part includes the total purchase price, and the financial terms and conditions of how the purchase price will be paid; including the mortgages, whether the buyer will get a new loan, take over the existing loan; also the down payment, who (buyer or seller) will pay which closing costs, and any shortage current at closing. In the absence of an escrow account, taxes shall be prorated as of the date of closing.

Part 3   This part includes all the standard clauses found in most purchase and sale contracts. They may vary from state-to-state, but all states usually include the following clauses:

A. Liquidation clause. This clause states what happens if the buyer does not close on the deal.

B. Wood destroying organisms report. This is sometimes referred to as "termite letter". When you're purchasing investment property, many times it will state in the special stipulations section that you are purchasing the property "as against" and there will be no termite letter provided by the seller.

C. Title examination and time for closing. This clause will be in every real estate contract somewhere. For the contract to be valid, it must indicate a termination date—usually the closing date.

D. Miscellaneous clauses. These may describe the property's condition at the time of closing, and who was responsible for the property prior to closing. These clauses are as follows:

   1. Loss or damage clause. In case of a fire prior to closing, who will be responsible for paying the damages;

   2. Disposition of personal property. At the time of closing, who will take possession of personal property;

   3. Occupancy clause. Who is currently residing in the property? Who may think the buyer illegally moved into the property?

   4. Zoning restrictions. This clause simply states what zoning laws apply to the property;

   5. Assignment of contract clause. As an investor, you will want all of your contracts to contain this clause. This clause says that you could designate a contract assignment, if you so chose. Which means, if you couldn't come up with the money to close on the property, you could assign the contract to another investor, and perhaps charge him or her a certain amount for that assignment (the only caveat to this assignment would be if the latter would not allow it).

E. Special stipulations clause. These are additional terms, conditions and exhibits. This is a section where you would write in your contingencies for the contract. For example, "This agreement is contingent upon my general contractor's inspection and approval of the property, within seven days of acceptance of the contract by the seller".

FYI: The 411 about Liquidated Damages

In most of the United States, the amount for liquidated damages is restricted to the amount of the earnest money deposit. This simply means that if you put in an offer to buy a property and you put up $500 earnest money, you can only lose $500 if you fail to close on that deal.

Part 4   The Last part of the purchase and sales agreement states that it is a legally binding agreement, and that you should seek legal consultation before signing it. It further stipulates that the laws of whatever state noted in the Agreement, govern the contract.

Last, but not least, there is the signature section that is always dated, and sometimes requires that you fill in a time, address, social security number (or Tax ID number), and any other data that realtors deem necessary.

As stated earlier, there are different contracts to sell and buy property. However, the contracts are the same, except for the wording of a few clauses. In the sales contract, for instance, as the seller YOU dictate certain considerations.

Think About It!

Learn as much as you can about the legalities of Real Estate Investing. Realtors, acting as a seller's agent, use contracts written for the benefit of the seller. The agent has a "FIDUCIARY" responsibility to the "SELLER'S BEST INTEREST". They are required under law to honor this responsibility. Therefore you, as the investor and the buyer, must look out for your own "BEST INTEREST".

Sample Real Estate Forms

Several forms have been provided in this section, to be used as examples only.

We don't recommend purchasing your real estate forms from the local office store. Attend your local real estate association and ask someone where you can get good, legal forms. The forms used in this book are excellent examples. However, laws might be slightly different in each state, so you need to purchase forms to conduct business in your state or go online to www.businessjumpstartseries.com for further information or forms.

SELLER INFORMATION CALL SHEET
Telephone Strategy

Date: Person's Name:
Realtor's Company   Is It Vacant?
Phone number

Hello, my name is _____ . I'm calling about your ad (or sign) that reads
_____ (key words).

Exactly where is it? _____

What is the address? _____

What cross streets is it near? _____

What is the price of the house? _____ Has the house been appraised? _____

How large is the house? _____

How many bedrooms and baths does it have? Bedrooms _____ Baths _____

What is the kitchen like? _____

What style is the house? _____

Does it have a view? _____ Is there a pool? _____

How old is the house? _____ What kind of heat does it have? _____

Is there air conditioning? _____ Are there repairs that need to be made? _____

Have there been estimates of what those repairs will cost? _____

How large is the lot? _____ What is it zoned for? _____

What kind of financing does the house have now? _____

How much is the 1st mortgage now? _____ Has owner looked into refinancing

that mortgage? _____ What is the interest rate on it? _____ For how

long? _____ How much are the monthly payments on the 1st mortgage? _____

Are there other mortgages on it now? _____ 2nd mortgage balance _____

interest rate _____ monthly payment _____ for how long _____

3rd mortgage balance _____ interest rate _____ monthly payment _____

for how long _____ Would the owner be willing to carry a mortgage for part of

the price? _____ How much? _____ at what interest? _____

How long _____ What kind of payment terms is owner looking for? _____

✳ How much cash do the owners need out of the sale? _____ Gee, why do they

need that much? _____

What are they going to do with the money? _____

Why are they selling? _____

Where are they moving to? _____

How soon are they going? _____ What kind of business did you say the owner is

in? _____ When can I see the house? _____

Is it vacant? _____ How soon can it be vacant? _____

How soon can they close escrow? _____ I'll drive by to see the outside

and call you back if I'm interested. Thank you for spending so much time talking to me.

CASH FLOW ANALYSIS

Gross Income:

Estimated Annual Gross Income
Other Income
Total Gross Income
Less Vacancy Allowance
Effective Gross Income

Expenses:

Taxes
Insurance
Water/Sewer
Garbage
Electricity
Licenses
Advertising
Supplies
Maintenance
Lawn
Snow Removal
Pest Control
Management (Off Site)
Management (On Site)
Accounting/Legal
Miscellaneous
Gas
Telephone
Pool
Elevator
Budget For Replacements

Total Expenses

Net Operating Income

Debt Service:

1 st Mortgage
2nd Mortgage
3rd Mortgage

Total Debt Service

Cash Flow:

Quick Check Inspection List

Electric

1. Turn on and off every light switch in house. Check for malfunctions. If bulbs don't light have seller change bulb to make sure circuit/switch is all right.

2. Look for dangling wires or broken sockets.

3. Check circuit breakers on fuse box. See if set up is modern (100 amp) or better.

   If house has old fashioned fuse box 30 or 60 amp circuits you will have to re-wire for modern heavy duty appliances.

4. Check to see. if they have enough wall plugs per room. One per room is inadequate, should have at least one outlet per wall, more often two per wall.

Plumbing

1. Turn on and off every faucet. Check for water pressure, it should be strong and fast. Check time necessary for hot water to become hot, should be hot in about 25 seconds, otherwise you have malfunctioning or inadequate water heater. If you have hot water but a low pressure the pipes are probably stopped up by mineral deposits.

2. Flush all toilets, *check for* pressure and time for tank to refill. Tank should refill within 3 minutes. In each bathroom, flush toilet and turn on all faucets full force at same time. If waste pipe is clogging, dark muck will then come into bath or shower drain.

3. Check for leaking in pipes etc.

4. Turn on and check all outside faucet/hose connections. Check for pressure and flow.

5. Turn on all sprinklers and look for dry spots in sprinkle pattern indicating broken sprinklers.

Gas

1. Turn on stove, ensure all burners work—if not check to seek if there is gas to stove or if burner is just stopped up.

2. Check furnace turn on and see if it lights right away—if not check pilot, gas connection or electronic ignition switch (if new furnace).

Structure

1. Walk entire floor. Check for springy or spongy spots in floor or any feeling of a section being inconsistent with rest of floor. If not right, peel carpet and check floor.

Roof

1. Look closely from ground for missing shingles or signs of damage, or spray with hose and check for leaks.

Appliances

1. Check all appliances, dishwasher, built in oven, air conditioning, for working condition.

Carpets

1. Check for rips, tears, or stains.

Exterior

1. Check for broken or torn screens, damaged wails interior or exterior. Check exterior light fixtures for missing parts. Notice whether door bell works.

ESTIMATING REHABILITATION COST USING CONTRACTORS
KEN JORDAN METHOD
(Similar Costs Apply to "Do It Yourself" if Inexperienced - ha! ha!)

ROOFING: $1.00 per square foot + $500 _____

WINDOWS & DOORS: $150 per unit - installed _____

LANDSCAPING: $300 but if earth moving equipment necessary $1000 _____

GUTTERING: $5.00 per linear foot _____

VINYL SIDING: $3,000 - $4,000 for average 2 - 3 bedroom home _____

KITCHEN UPDATE: $1,000 small but $2,000 or more if large or luxury _____

BATHROOM UPDATE: $1,000 unless luxury _____

CARPET: $1.00 per square foot - good quality installed _____

HARDWOOD FLOORS: $2.00 per square foot - high quality _____

PLUMBING: $1,000 replace galvanized pipe throughout average home _____

ELECTRICAL: $1,000 new panel;$2,000 full upgrade to 150 amp service _____

DRY BASEMENT: $3,000 for guaranteed job _____

FURNACE: $2,000 for complete update (easy access) _____

AIR CONDITIONING: $2,000 add to existing heat (easy access) _____

PAINTING - INTERIOR: $100 per room _____

PAINTING - EXTERIOR: $1,000 trim brick home or paint siding _____

LABOR: Skilled, licensed, bonded craftsperson with one helper-$300/day _____

MISC:_____

TOTAL REPAIR COSTS _____
FILE: BOOTESTI.CWK

PROPERTY ACQUISITION COSTS
Address_____

_____
(ARV) After repair value

A. Pre closing costs
    1. Earnest money deposit
    2. Appraisal
    3. Down payment
    4. Misc

    5. Total Pre-closing costs   -

B. Closing Costs (POC)
    6. Purchase closing costs
    7. Termite Letter
    8. Insurance Hazard)
    9. Pre-paids (Property taxes, Ins)
    10. Misc
    11. Total closing costs   -

C. Repair/ renovation costs
    12. Estimated repair budget
    13. Misc
    14. Total Fix-up costs   -

Total Holding costs
    15. Payments ___ Month PITI
    16. Total Holding Costs   -

E Sale/rental costs
    17. Renal /Management costs
    18. Sales Comisson Costs
    19. Advertising
    20. Total Sales/Rental Costs   -

ARV/ALES PRICE   +

Subtract Total of all costs (#5,11,14,16,20)   -
Subtract Mortgage Payoff(s)   -

**ESTIMATED NET PROFIT   . **

Real Estate Purchase and Sales Agreement

SELLER _____ **Phone** _____
Whos
BUYER _____ **Phone** _____

PROPERTY: Address: _____
LEGAL DESCRIPTION: Lot _____ Block _____ Subdivision_____
City _____, County _____

TERMS:
Cash paid at Closing	$ _____
Sum of all financing	$ _____
Subject to Existing Financing	$ _____
Total Purchase Price	$ _____

NO COSTS TO THE SELLER
Buyer will pay for all closing costs including the preparation of the documents, for the recording the deed, for title insurance.

PRORATIONS:
Real property taxes and rents will be prorated based on the current years tax without allowance for discounts or other exemptions.

CONVEYANCE:
Fee simple title to the property will be delivered to the Buyer, or to the Buyers assigns, by a General Warranty Deed free from any liens, restrictions, encumbrances, easements or encroachments not specifically referenced in this contract.

DEFECTS:
Seller warrants the property to be free from hazardous substances and from any violation of zoning, environmental, building, health or other governmental codes or ordinances and that there are no known facts regarding this property that could adversely affect its value.

NO JUDGMENTS:
Seller warrants that them are no judgments threatening the equity in subject properly, and that there is no bankruptcy pending or contemplated by any title-holder.

POSSESSION:
Possession of the property and occupancy (tenants excepted), with all keys and garage door openers, will be delivered to the Buyer when title transfers unless vacant. If vacant, possession and keys to the property will be given to Buyer upon execution of Contract. Leases, advance rents and security deposits will transfer to the Buyer with title.

"AS IS' and INSPECTIONS
This contract is contingent upon the Buyer's inspection and approval of subject property prior to transfer of title. The Seller agrees to provide access to the subject property to the Buyer's representatives, with power and utilities on, prior to transfer of title. If accepted property will convey in "AS IS" condition.

RIGHT TO ASSIGN
Contract may be assigned by Buyer's partner(s). If assigned, all rights, privileges and responsibilities under this contract will be assigned and Buyer will be relieved of same.

SPECIAL PROVISIONS
_____
_____
_____
_____

CLOSING will take place on or before: _____ at _____
Who's address is _____ phone _____

TIME IS OF THE ESSENCE of this agreement. Each contingency contained herein will be satisfied by the closing date or this contract extends to provide time for satisfaction of said contingencies. This offer expires if not accepted before: _____

BUYER: _____ Date_____

SELLER: _____ Date_____

SELLER _____ Date_____

LETTER OF INTENT TO PURCHASE REAL ESTATE

Property Address _____

Date_____

I 'm offering to purchase your property under the following terms and conditions:

_____

_____

_____

_____

_____

Sincerely,

Purchaser

AFFIDAVIT AND MEMORANDUM OF
AGREEMENT CONCERNING REAL ESTATE

State of _____
County of _____

BEFORE ME, the undersigned authority, on this day personally appeared _____, who being first duly sworn, deposes and says that:

1.   An agreement for the Purchase and Sale of the real property described in the attached Exhibit "A" was entered into by and between the Affiant, as Buyer, and _____, as Seller, on the _____ day of _____, 19___.

2.   The closing of the purchase and sale of said real property, per the terms of the Agreement, is to take place on or before the _____ day of _____, 19____.

3.   A copy of the agreement for purchase and sale of said real property may be obtained by contacting _____, whose mailing address is _____ _____, and whose telephone number is _____.

Dated this _____ day of _____, 19___.

FURTHER AFFIANT SAYETH NOT.

Signed, sealed and delivered
in the presence of:

_____   _____
WITNESS   AFFIANT

_____
WITNESS

Sworn to and subscribed before me this _____ day of _____, 19____

_____
(Seal)   NOTARY PUBLIC   STATE OF _____
                                My commission expires _____

This instrument was prepared by:
_____
_____
_____

EXHIBIT "A"
DESCRIPTION OF REAL PROPERTY

AFFIDAVIT AND MEMORANDUM OF AGREEMENT

State of
County of

        BEFORE ME, the undersigned authority, on this day personally appeared who being first duly sworn, deposes and says that:

1. An agreement for (Purchase or Sale, Lease-Option or Contract for Deed) of the real property described in Exhibit A was entered into by and between the affiant as (buyer or seller, optionor or optionee, lessor or leasee) on the   day of *(Mo.)*   , *(yr.)* .

2. If it is a sale or purchase, the closing of the purchase (or sale) of the said real property, per the terms of the Agreement, is to take place on or before the   day of *(Mo.)*   , *(yr.)*

Dated this   day of (mo.)   , (yr.)

Tax Code Number

FURTHER AFFIANT SAYETH NOT

        Signed, sealed and delivered in the presence of:

WITNESS   AFFIANT

WITNESS

Sworn to and described before me this   day of (mo.) ,
(yr.)

        (Seal)

                      NOTARY PUBLIC

                      STATE OF

                      My commission expires

QUIT CLAIM DEED

THE GRANTOR,_____ of _____,
City of _____, County of _____,
State of _____, for the consideration of _____
_____
CONVEY _____ and QUIT CLAIM _____ to _____
of _____, City of _____, County of _____
State of _____, all interest in the following described real estate
situated in the County of _____, in the State of _____, to wit:

Dated this _____ day of *(mo.)*_____, *(yr.)*_____.

_____
Grantor's Signature

_____
Type or Print Name

_____
Grantor's Signature

_____
Type or Print Name

STATE OF _____
COUNTY OF _____

I, _____, Notary Public in and for the state of
_____, do hereby certify that on this _____ day of *(mo.)*_____,
*(yr.)*_____, personally appeared before me _____
known to be the individual described in and who executed the within instrument and
acknowledged that _____ signed the same as _____
free and voluntary act and deed for the uses and purposes herein mentioned.

Given under my hand and official seal this _____ day of *(mo.)*_____,
(yr.) _____. Commission expires *(mo./day)*_____, *(yr.)* _____.

_____
Notary Public

CLOSING STATEMENT

PROPERTY _____   BROKER _____
_____   PURCHASER_____
SELLER _____   ADDRESS _____
ADDRESS_____   _____
_____   DATE OF CONTRACT_____
DATE OF CLOSING _____   DATE FOR POSSESSION_____

	CREDIT PURCHASER		CREDIT SELLER	
Purchase Price				
Earnest Money				
First Mortgage				
Interest (_____ days @ $ _____ per day)				
Second Mortgage				
Interest (_____ days @ $ _____ per day)				
General Taxes (yr.) _____				
General Taxes (yr.) _____				
(prorated from _____ to _____)				
Special Assessments				
Insurance Premium, Unearned				
Rents (from _____ to _____)				
Utilities (from _____ to _____)				
Check Or Cash To Balance				
TOTAL				

SETTLEMENT	DEBIT		CREDIT	
Balance As Above				
Earnest Money				
Abstract Or Guaranty Policy				
Recording Fees				
Commission				
Balance				
TOTAL				

Accepted: Accepted:

_____   _____
Signature   Signature

_____   _____
Signature   Signature

BILL OF SALE

Seller,   , of   , in
consideration of _   dollars, receipt whereof
is hereby acknowledged, does hereby sell, assign, transfer, and set over to Buyer,
                                                                          of
                                   the following described personal property, to-wit:
Seller hereby represents and warrants to Buyer that Seller is the absolute owner of said property, that said property is free and clear of all liens, charges, and encumbrances, and that Seller has full right, power, and authority to sell said personal property and to make this bill of sale. All warranties of quality, fitness, and merchantability are hereby excluded.

if this bill of sale is signed by more than one person, all persons so signing shall be jointly and severally bound hereby.
IN WITNESS WHEREOF, Seller has signed and sealed this bill of sale at
day of (mo.)   , (yr.) -

DEPOSIT NOTE

$ _____   Date _____

_____ days after the above date, the undersigned promises to pay to the order of
_____, the sum of _____
dollars ($ _____), without interest, payable at _____.

In the event that this note is not paid when due and suit is instituted for the collection
thereof, the undersigned promises to pay to the holder of this note reasonable attorney
fees for making such collection.

_____
Signature

This note is given as a deposit in connection with the agreement between _____
_____ and _____,
dated _____ , covering the real property or premises commonly known
as _____.

This note is void unless said agreement is accepted according to its terms.

INSTALLMENT NOTE

$ _____   City _____ , State _____

                          Date _____ , (yr.) _____

FOR VALUE RECEIVED, the undersigned (Borrower) promises to pay to the order of
_____ , the principal sum of _____ dollars, with
interest on the unpaid principal balance from the date of this Note, until paid, at the rate of
_____ percent per annum. Principal and interest shall be payable at
_____ , or such other place as the Note holder may designate, in consecu-
tive monthly installments of _____ dollars ($ _____) on the _____ day
of each month beginning _____ , (yr.) _____ . Such monthly installments shall
continue until entire indebtedness evidenced by this Note is fully paid, except that any remaining
indebtedness, if not sooner paid, shall be due and payable on _____ .

If any monthly installment under this Note is not paid when due and remains unpaid after a date specified by a notice to Borrower, the entire principal amount outstanding and accrued interest thereon shall
at once become due and payable at the option of the Note holder. The date specified shall not be less
than thirty (30) days from the date such notice is mailed. The Note holder may exercise this option to
accelerate during any default by borrower regardless of any prior forbearance. If suit is brought to
collect this Note, the Note holder shall be entitled to collect all reasonable costs and expenses of suit,
including, but not limited to, reasonable attorney fees.

Borrower shall pay to the Note holder a late charge of five percent (5%) of any monthly installment not
received by the Note holder within ten (10) days after the installment is due.

Borrower may prepay the principal amount outstanding, in whole or in part, at any time, and without penalty.

Presentment, notice of dishonor, and protest are hereby waived by all makers, sureties, guarantors,
and endorsers hereof. This Note shall be the joint and several obligation of all makers, sureties, guarantors, and endorsers, and shall be binding upon them and their successors and assigns.

Any notice to Borrower provided for in this Note shall be given by mailing such notice by certified mail
addressed to Borrower or to such other address as Borrower may designate by notice to the Note
holder. Any notice to the Note holder shall be given by mailing such notice by certified mail, return
receipt requested, to the Note holder at the address stated in the first paragraph of this Note, or at such
other address as may have been designated by notice to Borrower.

This indebtedness evidenced by this Note is secured by a Deed of Trust or Mortgage dated
_____ , and reference is made to the Deed of Trust or Mortgage for rights as to
acceleration of the indebtedness evidenced by this Note.

_____
Signature of Borrower

_____
Address

_____

PROMISSORY NOTE

FOR VALUE RECEIVED, _____ **of**

ADDRESS: _____, CITY: _____, STATE: _____ ZIP: _____,

promise(s) to pay to the order of _____ **the**

principal sum of _____ **and /100 DOLLARS ($** _____ **), in legal tender of the United States, with interest from the date hereof at the rate of ____% per year or any part thereof. Should this Note be paid in full within thirty days from the date hereof or at any time during a thirty day period, interest shall be charged at a daily rate of $_____ per day.**

Principal and interest shall be payable at the offices of:

or at such other place as the holder hereof may designate in writing.

Should any installment not be paid when due, or should the Maker or Makers hereof fail to comply with any of the terms of this agreement, or if Holder deems itself insecure or if Maker defaults under these terms, the entire unpaid principal sum evidenced by this Note, with all agreed interest, shall, at the option of the Holder, and without notice to the undersigned, become due and may be collected forthwith, time being of the essence of this Agreement. It is further agreed that failure of the Holder to exercise this right of accelerating the maturity of the debt, or indulgence granted from time to time, shall in no event be considered as a waiver of such right of acceleration or estop the Holder from exercising such right.

Installments, or payment if single payment Note, not paid within 5 days of due date shall incur a late fee of 15% of the installment or payment, but not less than $10.00. The Holder shall be entitled to all costs of collection should this Note, or any part of the indebtedness evidenced hereby, be accelerated and not paid. Should this note be collected at law or by an attorney at law, an Attorney/Collection Fee of 15% of the balance due, but not less than $100.00, plus any costs and administration fees, shall be added.

And each of the undersigned, whether principal, surety, guarantor, endorser, or other party, severally waives and renounces demand, protest, notice of demand, protest and non-payment.

IN WITNESS WHEREOF, the parties hereto have caused these presents to be signed in person this _____ day of _____, 19____.

_____   _____(SEAL)
Witness
                                                        Social Security #: _____

_____   _____(SEAL)
Notary Public
                                                        Social Security #: _____

PAYMENT SCHEDULE:

DATE DUE	AMOUNT	DATE DUE	AMOUNT	DATE DUE	AMOUNT
_____	_____	_____	_____	_____	_____
_____	_____	_____	_____	_____	_____
_____	_____	_____	_____	_____	_____
_____	_____	_____	_____	_____	_____

WRAP-AROUND MORTGAGE AND SECURITY AGREEMENT

THIS MORTGAGE is made and entered into this _____ day of _____, 19 _____, by and between _____ whose address is _____, (hereinafter referred to as "Mortgagor") and _____, whose address is _____, (hereinafter referred to as "Mortgagee").

THIS IS A WRAP-AROUND MORTGAGE SUBJECT TO THAT CERTAIN MORTGAGE HERETOFORE EXECUTED IN FAVOR OF _____, DATED THE ___ DAY OF ___, 19_, AND RECORDED IN OFFICIAL RECORDS BOOK _____, PAGE _____, ON THE _____ DAY OF _____, 19 _____, IN THE ORIGINAL PRINCIPAL AMOUNT OF _____ Dollars ($ _____).

Mortgagor agrees to comply with all the terms and conditions of the above described mortgage, including, but not limited to, those concerning taxes and insurance, other than with respect to the payment of principal or interest due under said mortgage. If Mortgagor herein shall fail to comply with all the terms, provisions and conditions of said mortgage so as to result in a default thereunder (other than with respect to payments of principal or interest due), that failure on the part of Mortgagor herein shall constitute a default under this Mortgage and shall entitle Mortgagee herein, at its option, to exercise any and all rights and remedies given the Mortgagee in the event of a default under this Mortgage.

Mortgagor and Mortgagee hereby covenant and agree not to enter into any agreement with the holder of the above described Mortgage, modifying or amending any of the provisions dealing with payment of principal or interest under said Mortgage without the prior written consent of the other.

If the Mortgagee hereunder shall default in making any required payment of principal or interest under the above described mortgage, the Mortgagor shall have the right to advance funds necessary to cure that default and all funds so advanced by Mortgagor shall be credited against the next installment of principal and interest due under the Note secured by this Mortgage.

WITNESSETH, that in consideration of the premises and in order to secure the payment of both the principal and interest and any other sums payable on the note (as hereinafter defined) or this Mortgage and the performance and observance of all of the provisions hereof and of said note, Mortgagor hereby grants, sells, warrants, conveys, assigns, transfers, mortgages, and sets over unto Mortgagee, all of Mortgagor's estate, right, title and interest in, to and under all that certain real property situate in the County of _____, State of _____, more particularly described in Exhibit "A", attached hereto and made a part hereof, together with all buildings, structures and improvements of every nature whatsoever, now or hereafter located on said real property and all fixtures, appliances, apparatus, equipment, furnishings, heating and air conditioning equipment, machinery and articles of personal property and replacement thereof (other than those owned by lessees of said real property) now or hereafter affixed to, attached to, placed upon, or used in any way in connection with the complete and comfortable use, occupancy, or operation of the said real property, all licenses and permits used or required in connection with the use of said real property, all leases of said real property now or hereafter entered into and all right, title and interest of Mortgagor thereunder, including, without limitation, cash or securities deposited thereunder pursuant to said leases, and all rents, issues, proceeds, and profits from said real property and together with all proceeds of the conversion, voluntary or involuntary, of any of the foregoing into cash or liquidated claims, including, without limitation, proceeds of insurance and condemnation awards. The foregoing real property and tangible and intangible personal property are hereinafter referred to collectively as the "Mortgaged Property".

Joint Venture Agreement

A. **Parties of the Joint Ventrure.** <u>Entities</u> This joint venture agreement is between , '-LC (hereinafter refered to as party of the lst part) and ., LLC (hereinafter referred to as party of the 2nd part) and is based on the following:

B. **Terms of this agreement** 1. .ʳ .LLC shall provide a credit worthy party to ultimately purchase the deal and provide an upfront portion of the funding to secure deal. (See disbursement of funds section below).

2.   ~., LLC shall provide services I-IV on the information sheet, I propert Locator service
II Deal Assessment service, III. Property acquisition service and IV Light rehab and repair
Service (see sheet attached) V sale and or rental service would require a separate agreement
And is not a part of this deal.

C. Disbursement of funds The following costs will be divided 50/50 % between both entities (See property Acquisition costs A-D)(<u>Note</u>: . Will provide 1 month Mortgage and will pay it directly from the. ~ _ Account). Pre- closing costs will be paid upfront prior to closing split 50/50. The balance of the costs will be substracted from the sale and the balance of the funds will be divided 50/50 % between entities and paid immediately after closing. Each entity will be responsible for it's own taxes. One entity may prepare a 1098 for the other entity as necessary.

D. Property ownership Once the closing has occured and all parties have been paid the 100% property ownership shall remain with the party of the first part of the joint venture with all the rights and responsibilities therof.

There are no other agreements , promises or understandings between the parties except as specifically set forth herein. This legal and binding Agreement will be constued under <u>Georgia</u> Law.

IN WITNESS WHEREOF, all of the parties hereto affix their hands and seals on the day of , 2002

Party I   , LLC   Party II '   , LLC

Party I   , LLC

The ultimate of being successful is the luxury of
giving yourself the time to do what you want to do."
—Leontyne Price

Chapter 6

Assembling your Dream Team

There are several tools involved in putting together a profitable real estate transaction. In order to build a thriving and successful Real Estate Investment Business, you must also have what is called your "Dream Team". So, whether you are going to buy, sell and/or rehab real estate, these people will support you in your real estate investment efforts.

Your key team members should include:

▼ **Real Estate Agent**—a Person licensed by the state in which they practice to assist people in the purchase and sale of their property for a commission

▼ **Real Estate Attorney**—an Attorney who specializes in real estate transactions.

▼ **Mortgage Broker** —a Person who works on funding side of the real estate business securing loans for buyers from various lenders

▼ **Appraiser**—A Person who requires specialized training and an apprenticeship for so many hours. You can work for lenders, corporations, private individuals, or real estate agents.

▼ **General Contractor**—a Person who itemizes the needed repair work on a rehab property and subsequently hires and supervises a professional staff to do those repairs.

▼ **Mentor/Role Model**—a Mentor can be a friend, family member, coach, teacher, guru—someone who provides unwavering support and guidance to help you to be the best that you can be. A good place to find a mentor who can help you with your real estate investment business is at your local real estate association.

Role models, unlike mentors, are people who are (or were) examples of success in their chosen field. These are the people you should study and choose to follow. How do you find role models? Do your homework on that person's life and history, and find out everything you can about them. Use what you learn to help you build your successful Real Estate Investment Business.

Do Your Homework!

Here are some general questions you can ask potential team members:

Q1. Have you worked with real estate investors before? For how long?

Q2. Do your own your own home?

Q3. Do you own any investment property?

Q4. Have you attended or participated in any real estate investing seminars?

Q5. How familiar are you with the farming area? How long have you worked and/or lived in that area?

There are many others that you can (and probably will) bring into your team. However, the group listed above is what you will need to help you get started. They are not listed in order of importance, but eventually, you will need each of them in some capacity to help you complete your real estate transactions.

There are people you will, and people you will not be able to work with. So, be very careful when choosing your team. You'll need to find people that are experienced in those particular areas. So, choose only those who compliment your business needs and your personality.

And, keep in mind also that your team may fluctuate as you start making different types of real estate transactions.

For example, you may find a deal in which you can buy a discounted note, or a deal where you can buy a mobile home. Or, here's an attention-grabbing flyer from a Real Estate Company that handles foreclosed properties—you can try something similar.

FORECLOSED PROPERTY

"Someone else's loss is your gain!!!"

123 Anywhere Avenue, Atlanta 30001

RENT IS CURRENTLY $400/MONTH FROM STABLE
MONTH-TO-MONTH TENANTS
TENANT WILL LEAVE UPON REQUEST

$69.9K OR BEST OFFER

▼ HARD MONEY FINANCING ALREADY IN PLACE
▼ N0 ORIGINATION FEES OR POINTS
▼ LENDER IS ANXIOUS TO SELL

Sales in past year within 1/2 mile radius

ADDRESS	SQUARE FOOT	SALES PRICE	SALES DATE
1008 Hollywood Rd.	896	$132,000	July, 2002
2266 Kennedy Ct.	1,080	$122,000	July, 2002
754 Cedar Ave.	1,104	$115,500	June 2002
675 Cedar Ave.	1,032	$113,000	August 2002

DIRECTIONS: From 285 - Exit US 78/Bankhead Highway. Turn Left onto US 78/Bankhead Highway. Turn Left onto Center Hill Avenue. Drive-by and if you're interested, we will arrange a walk through with the tenants.

CALL: BEST REAL ESTATE INVESTMENTS

555-5555

Try these Great Resources and Marketing Ideas to Enhance your Real Estate Investment Business:

▼ **Attorneys:** Those who handle divorces, probates and real estate closings, have information on motivated sellers and may share this information with other clients.

▼ **Real Estate Newsletters:** Potentially you can find wholesale properties offered by other investors in your area.

▼ **Foreclosure Hot Sheets:** Subscribe to foreclosure hot sheets, a collection of compiled information of all the foreclosures in your county, and in your state.

▼ **HUD and VA Properties:** You can find information regarding these properties on the Internet.

▼ **Business Cards and Flyers:** This is an inexpensive way to advertise. Make sure your cards and flyers say, "I buy houses".

▼ **Real Estate Auctions:** When you participate in purchasing property this way, you really must know the true value of the home. Oftentimes, people overbid properties.

▼ **Classified Advertising:** You can place your own ads saying that you purchase properties. Make sure to list your telephone number.

▼ **Magnetic Signs:** Put magnetic signs on all of your vehicles. It should say, "I buy houses", and your phone number.

▼ **Door Hangers:** Hire a service to place door hangers in your farming neighborhood, stating that you're interested in purchasing properties.

▼ **T-shirts:** T-shirts made with your name and number.

▼ **Yard Signs:** Place these signs in high traffic areas. It should say that you buy houses with your phone number listed.

▼ **Direct Mail:** Prepare a flyer and place in direct mail pieces (sometimes called piggy-back mail).

▼ **Contracted Builders:** Builders can be a great source for referrals. Sometimes they're even willing to sell their properties at cost.

▼ **Corporate Communications:** Many large companies have their own in-house newsletters and bulletin boards. These are good places to reach employees, or those being transferred or laid off.

▼ **Telemarketers:** Hire telemarketers to talk with potential sellers. Get contact information from newspapers, expired realtor listing books, and other sources from which you can get telephone numbers.

▼ **Tax rolls:** The county courthouse has records on properties that have defaulted on their taxes. You can get this list of the property owners (public record) and mail letters to them asking if they're willing to sell.

▼ **Radio Spots:** You can run a 40-60 second commercial saying that you buy properties.

▼ **Exhibitions:** There are several show exhibitions being held around the country. You can purchase a booth, offer a free drawing, and talk to people who may be interested in selling their homes.

▼ **Sponsor a Little League Team:** Put your business name, address, and phone number on team T-shirts, stating that you buy houses.

▼ **Billboards:** Sometimes for a nominal fee, you can rent a billboard by the side of a highway or road and advertise your business.

▼ **Voice mail:** Set up a pre-recorded message that gives away free reports and takes information from people who might be interested in selling their homes.

▼ **Bus Benches:** Many bus stop park benches have space available for advertising. Keep your ad to a simple call for action, including your phone number.

▼ **"For Sale by Owner" Magazines:** This is a great avenue for running an "I buy and/or lease houses". In addition, you could offer a free report.

▼ **Mailman:** Oftentimes, the first person to know about a vacant house is the mailman. However, you will have to develop a relationship with them before they are willing to share information.

▼ **Neighbors:** Every neighborhood has one or two people that "know" the neighborhood, including who is moving and why. Get to know these neighbors.

Think About It!

In addition to assembling your team members, consider other ways to increase your options for buying and selling. Remember, use OPE (other people's experiences) and resources and before you know it, you'll be an expert at making $30,000 in 30 days.

> *"Most people search high and wide for the key to success...
> if they only knew the key to their dreams lies within."*
> —George Washington Carver

Chapter 7
Achieving Your Dream

"Do you have a dream?"

Every major accomplishment known to man began in someone's mind as a thought or a dream; and it is probable that it was written down. It is important for you to sit down and ask yourself, "What is my dream?" "When I'm 90 years old, sitting in my rocking chair, what is it I want to say that I accomplished?" Write it down. The most famous African-American dreamer was Dr. Martin Luther King Jr. In his "I have a dream" speech, Dr. King wrote and described his dream—the right to equality—and he realized it through his "non-violence" movement (he took action).

Other examples of African-American dreamers are: Harriet Tubman and her dream to lead as many slaves to freedom as she could through the Underground Railroad; Madame C. J. Walker and her dream to provide Black Hair Care Products to African Americans.

Take Note:
There are many African-Americans who gained both success and fame through their dreams—and it's a fact in history that they took action to realize them. They all wrote down their dreams in detail—they made a plan for their success!

What does it take for you to do what you truly want to do? What would you have to do to do it? For example, if you're planning to travel around the world, you must first create a budget and then map out different routes. How much money will it take? Can you afford the time?

I want you to take a minute and write out a paragraph (three or four sentences in your journal), addressing this hypothetical question.

The reason for this exercise is to get you to a point where you can at least be honest with yourself and see what it would really take to accomplish this goal. After you finish, put your journal somewhere accessible so you can refer to it again and again.

You may ask yourself, "What does this have to do with the subject of a real estate investment business? The answer is **everything**. What we think about (dream about) **AND** write about, we bring about, and our priorities come first.

People need a strong enough "why" before they will take action. The same is true with real estate investing. There must be some aspect of the real estate investment business that appeals to you personally.

▼ Do you want to start a real estate investment business as a supplement to your current income?

▼ Are you interested in making this your career?

▼ Do you just want to try to find a house to live in?

▼ Do you like the idea of providing housing opportunities to a particular group?

▼ Do you want to provide jobs for housing contractors?

▼ Do you like the challenge of putting deals together in order to get paid handsomely for your endeavors?

▼ Do you want to become involved in the financing side of real estate and assist families in purchasing a home?

▼ Do you want to help your own family by providing additional income and teaching your children the importance of investing, thus providing them with another life skill?

Whatever it is, write it down.

Do Your Homework

Keep in mind that your dream must also connect to a budget plan to accomplish what you want to do in life. How much can you afford? Write it down.

Achieving Your DREAM

Let's begin with your BIG DREAM—This MUST be in writing. Below are the components.

- ▼ Your "Why" DREAM—Make it as big and as clear as possible.

- ▼ Your "What and When" GOAL—Make these "time" specific and "amount" specific.

- ▼ Your "Who and How" PLAN—Explain in detail how your goal is to be accomplished.

Test yourself. These following three tests are about mind management, time management, and money management (MTM):

1. Mind Management: The Test of Your Mind-set

What is your mind-set? —Prosperity vs. Poverty

I once heard Dr. Frederick Eikerenkoetter, better known as "Rev. Ike" say in one of his sermons, "*GOD answers prayer with good ideas. Whatever we think about we bring about*".

It's good to have a "prosperity mentality". There are many ways to enrich your mind and maintain those positive endorphins! For example, just to name a few, you can employ:
- ▼ Meditation
- ▼ Prayer
- ▼ Inspirational reading
- ▼ Nature walks
- ▼ Exercising

On the other hand, if you are always thinking about what you do not have, rather than what you do have, you are suffering from what is called "poverty mentality".

2. Time Management: The Test of Time
Can you find and/or commit to the time needed to run a real estate investment business?

All of us have the same amount of time (168 hours a week.). How that time is managed is the difference between just making it and becoming wealthy. Wealthy people manage their time effectively.

Unfortunately, many African Americans admit that they do not tend to use their time wisely, and therefore hold themselves back from achieving the wealth they desire.

Just a Thought!

Remember, Time Is Money! If you are stuck doing menial tasks, you're actually losing money.

Think about how your time is spent. After allowing time for sleep, travel, and your regular job, plus eating and personal hygiene, you will have approximately 40 hours remaining. This is not a lot of time, considering church and personal errands, plus your children's activities and your entertainment, etc.

Consider delegating certain activities. Realistically, if you want to have a part-time business, you will probably have to give something up. Are you willing to do that? You will also have to be willing to delegate certain activities. Have you ever considered delegating any job paying less than what you make per hour?

List your menial jobs. That would mean things like housecleaning, gardening, food, shopping, and other menial tasks should probably be delegated. Let's review the following chart, which is based upon income per hour. If you will notice, the column on the left is your total annual income. For example, let's say your total income is $35,000 a year at 40 hours per week. Your hourly wage is $17.50.

Who can you get to help out? Based on your goal of obtaining wealth, any job paying less than $17.50 per hour should be delegated. For instance, an administrative or executive assistant should handle secretarial type services, such as: answering phones, filing, sending out letters and making simple follow-up calls, etc. This will free your time to look at properties, make offers, and increase your income beyond our example of $17.50 per hour.

Total Annual Income in $	30 hours/week in $ per hour	40 Hours/week in $ per hour	50 Hours/week in $ per hour	60 Hours/week in $ per hour
20,000	13.34	10.00	8.00	5.67
25,000	16.67	12.50	10.00	8.34
30,000	20.00	15.00	12.00	10.00
35,000	23.34	17.50	14.00	11.67
40,000	26.67	20.00	16.00	13.34
50,000	33.34	25.00	20.00	16.67
60,000	40.00	30.00	24.00	20.00
75,000	20.00	37.50	30.00	25.00
100,000	56.67	50.00	40.00	33.34
150,000	100.00	75.00	60.00	50.00
200,000	133.34	100.00	80.00	56.67
300,000	200.00	150.00	120.00	100.00
400,000	266.67	200.00	160.00	133.34
500,000	333.34	250.00	200.00	166.67
Total #of hrs worked/year (50 weeks)	1,500	2,000	2,500	3,000

3. Money Management: The Test of Money Management

Can you manage your money if you don't get a paycheck every two weeks or every month?

It has been said many times "It's not the money you make. It's the money you keep." One definition of a MILLIONAIRE is one who has assets worth 1 million dollars or more after all debts are paid. The key is you must be able to invest enough to be able to have $1 million dollars, *above what you owe.*

Did You Know?

According to the Federal Reserve, over 40% of US families spend more than they earn. The average American household has 13 payment cards, including credit cards, debt cards and store cards. On average the typical credit card purchase is 112% higher than if using cash.

The problem is, most people make the $1 million dollars over their lifetime, but spend $1½ million dollars with the use of credit card debt.

I would be willing to bet that many of you reading this guide have or will earn a million dollars in your lifetime. Allow me to explain. Assume you and your spouse make $8.50 per hour or $17.00 per hour if you combine your wages. Over the course of a 40-hour workweek for 30 years—assuming that you worked at least fifty weeks a year—you would earn over $1,000,000 (one million dollars).

Let me show you the math:

$17.00 x 40 hours per week equals $680.00 per week. Multiply $680.00 x 52 weeks (1 year) and you'll make $35,360 per year. Your combined income of $35,360 per year x 30 years equals $1,060,800 (One Million, sixty thousand, eight hundred dollars). This amount is what you will have earned over the span of your employment.

Think About It!

When formulating your personal plans, always think of the highest and best use of your mind, time and money—your MTM. With this formula, you will be well on your way to building a successful Real Estate Investment Business.

Be the best you can be; do well or don't do it at all.
If you don't enjoy what you are doing, you won't do it well.
—Sylvia Woods

Chapter 8
Setting Your Goal...Working Your Plan

So, you've dreamed your dream. Now it's time to set your goal and work your plan of action.

Before we go forward, however, it is necessary to mention a subject that was mentioned in the Introduction...GUTS, or rather, Get Up and Tackle Something. In my first real estate seminar, the question was asked, "What's the most important characteristic needed to make money in real estate," and the answer was "Guts"? After 15 years, I still find this answer to be true. GUTS implies desire and commitment. In the following chapter, I'll discuss it in more detail, but for now, just know that it's something you really need to build your successful Real Estate Investment Business.

To achieve your dream, you need to set a specific goal and you need to be committed to attaining it. For example, you are 35 years old; and by age 60 you want to be a millionaire. To accomplish this, you would have to save or invest $40,000 at a conservative 8% per year. This $40,000 would have to be above and beyond your cost of living and your debts. Where are you right now in terms of this goal?

A reality check is required. You need to assess where you are right now and find out how close you are to attaining your annual goal. Begin by writing down how much debt do you owe?

▼ Using your credit report, make a list of your debts.
▼ After each credit card, list the interest rate.

▼ List your utility and phone bills, and the cost to purchase food and any other miscellaneous expenses that may not be reported on your credit report. This list will give you a clear picture of what you are paying out each month.

Next, use your paycheck stubs or your income statement (if you're in business) to break down your monthly income. Use your net income and subtract your expenditures for twelve months (Use your net operating income if you've been in business for twelve months). This figure represents your current net income.

Remember, I said this was a reality check. So, let's assess the situation. If this figure breaks even or has a negative balance, then you're spending more than you're earning and you will not meet your millionaire goal this year.

But, now that you know how to begin the process, give yourself a little time and gain as much knowledge on the subject as possible. You can do it!

On the other hand, if this figure is $40,000 or more, you're well on your way to your goal of $1 million dollars by age 60. Congratulations!! You're off to a great start.

Setting Goals

Something magical happens in the brain when the pen meets the paper. So, we are now going to discuss the process of setting goals. You must learn how to write an "implementation plan". In order to do this, the following questions should jump-start your thinking process.

This Is a Key Point: Your Plan Must Be in Writing. No exceptions!

Write down the overall goal for your Real Estate Investment Business? Such as:

▼ I want to finance my child's education within the next seven years, using my real estate investing; or

▼ I want to make $100,000 by the end of this year by flipping real estate homes.

▼ What appeals to you about the Real Estate Investment Business?

▼ Have you selected a geographical area to seek out real estate property?

▼ Are you familiar with your local real estate investing trade association?

▼ Why do you want a Real Estate Investment Business, versus continuing your current career path?

▼ Are you looking for a property to live in?

▼ Are you more interested in selling wholesale real estate wholesale or retail? Do you know the difference?

▼ Are you planning to invest in rentals and keep these properties for income?

▼ Have you written a budget (including staff, establishment)?

▼ Is your establishment properly equipped (computers, copy machines, etc.)?

▼ What specific skills and/or characteristics do you have that will enhance your Real Estate Investment Business?

▼ How does Real Estate Investing fit into your overall investment plan?

▼ Who specifically is supporting you in your Real Estate Investment Business goal (i.e. spouse, friends, business partner, children)?

▼ Do you know anyone successful in the Real Estate Investment Business that you can ask for advice?

Listing information is very helpful. It allows you to prioritize all of your options. To give you an idea, below is an action plan, based upon expressed, written goals.

Goal: To Earn $100,000 Within The Next 12 Months

The Implementation Plan: Why Do I Want This Goal?

You need to clearly understand the "why" for your specific goal. In this example, there are five reasons given for "why". However, you can have as many reasons as you want. Actually, the more reasons, the better. The more "whys" you have, the more compelled you are to reach you goal.

1. I don't want my parent's lifestyle (poverty mentality).

2. To live a retirement-type lifestyle (freedom of choice in all areas).

3. To pay off ALL creditors (approximately $30,000) and remain debt free.

4. To assist kids who have been severely abused and ignored by society.

5. To give back to the community by sharing my business skills with anyone; especially women, so they can always take care of themselves, whether they are single, divorced, widowed, or retired.

How Will I Reach This Goal?

Primary methods should be listed to answer "how" you will accomplish the goal. You need to list the ways and means in order to reach your income goal. For instance:

1) Real Estate investments (i.e. discounted mortgages, tax certificates, flippers).

2) Portfolio Income Method (Keep monies invested in high interest compounded accounts, through tools such as self-directed IRAs, Stocks, bonds, IRAs, Real Estate Investment Trusts (REIT) to purchase properties.

3) Business income method (Any established business that produces a steady stream of income).

Take Note!

Your goals must be clear and concise. You must validate the reasons for them (WHY). Don't be afraid to be as forthcoming as possible. The "HOW" is revealed when you order your priorities.

Marketing Strategy!

Let's say you decided that your goal would be best accomplished by doing a purchase and investment strategy. To complete the goal even faster, an "investment product business" strategy was simultaneously created.

Strategy 1: Proposed Real Estate Investment Earnings Plan
Strategy 2: Real Estate Investment Products Business Plan.

Activity or PERT Chart!

It is necessary to take each individual investment, product, and or service goal, and create a uniformed time-line for each necessary activity. For example, the chart below shows the beginning and end date of each activity. Most of the activities overlap in time, so if put on a graph, would look like a sliding scale.

STRATEGY–1: Proposed Real Estate Investment Earnings Plan

Date	Activity	Person	Responsible for Activity	Results
2/1- Ongoing	Attend monthly GAREIA meetings	Owner		Continue to build network
2/1-Ongoing	Get on Investor's fax lists	Owner/WP		Review several properties
3/1-Ongoing	Make list of vacant Properties	Owner/ Bird-dog		Make 4+ offers @wk
2/1-8/1	Look up tax properties at Courthouse	AA/ W/P		Send out letters and looked up phone numbers
4/1-6/1	Purchase foreclosure list/send letters	Owner/WP		Follow-up with phone calls and make offers
3/15-4/1	Do a search on Internet for properties	Owner/WP		Make offer
3/15-7/15	Attend GAREIA Sub Groups	Consultant/ Investors/Owner		Network, form partnerships/deals
3/15-7/15	Attend seminar on entity development	Owner/CPA		Set up business entities
3/1-8/1	Join other Real Estate Investment groups	Owner		Make offer such as L/O
2/1-8/1	Work one-on-one with my mentor/teacher	Owner/ mentor		Learn how to buy properties

STRATEGY—2: Real Estate Investment Products Business Plan
Product Lists For Real Estate Support Products & Services

Product Name	Description	Marketing Strategy*
1 "Appear Gear"	Color change paper and T-shirts (for advertising)	I, MO, DM, PR trade show
2 "BIZ BAGS"	Groups of published reports	MO, I, DM, R
3 Interactive Manual	Training & Biz Develop Manual	MO, CD, DM, R
4 RE Info store	Online Information store	I, PR, CD, MO, R
5 Individual reports	IE, Foreclosures, tax properties	CD, I, MO, R
6 Internet RE searches	Internet guide to online	RE I, MO, DM, PR, R
7 MLM Type programs	RE Licensing & distributorships	CD, DM, I, MO, R
8 Real Estate "FFIG"	Financial Flipper mentor course	PR to COLLEGES, R
9 Jumpstart	RE Course Seminar series	PR To Adult schools, R
10 GAREIA Course	Seminar for RE Assoc Members	PR Thru RE associations
11 Introductory Course	3 hour course general public	I, MO, DM, PR, R
12 RE Marketing course	For intermediate RE Investors	I, MO, DM, PR, R
13 Audio Cassette tapes	6 Tape introductory set	I, MO, DM, PR,
14 3 day Boot-Camp	Total RE Course in 1 weekend	I, MI, DM, PR, R
15 Special Forms CD	General Forms and my designs	I, MO, DM, PR, R
16 Real Estate E-zine	Internet monthly mailings	INTERNET, Affiliates
17 Private consultations	Telephone, e-mail, in person	CD, DM, I, MO, PR R

Note: Each product above needs a sales letter, an ad sheet and an order form

*DM=Direct Mail
*MO=Mail Order
*R=Referral

Once you have assessed what you have to work with, you can decide on a time-line. Look at each individual product and/or service, and determine what you need to do for each one. (The following example plan covers a six-month period.)

Marketing Campaign Over Next Six Months
(Pert Activity Chart)

Date(s)	Activity	Person responsible for activity	Results to date
2/1-4/1	Develop the following skills	Owner, consultants, WP	
			Contacted web developer
	1. Maintain web pages		Purchased E-mail software
	2. Bulk e-mail		Took an online seminar
	3. Internet ads		Advertising
	4. Database		
	5. Send Press Releases		
	6. Publish E-Books "		
2/1-3/30	1. Develop a minimum of 4 offers	Owner, Consultant	
	2. Prepare 3 ads per offer	Owner, Consultant	Purchase MS Publisher to
	3. Prepare Business cards	Owner, Partner	With development of Ads
	4. Send out ½ million e-mails	Owner& WP	Researched several companies
			that develop Admax Sites
2/15-3/15	Develop Admax Site	Owner and Admax	Set-up appt. w/consultant
2/1-3/30	Start building prospect list		That do online marketing
			(10,000 in 6 mo.) campaigns
Began 2/5	in Progress		
4/15/-6/15	Develop, send Press Releases	Owner, consultant &WP	Have put together some
			background information
	Begin development of the		
	Real Estate info Store "		
3/1-7/1	Place ads on 800 +Free sites	Owner & WP	Identified some good sites
			for my market for ads pay-per
			click sites, free e-zine, low
			cost print ads
2/1-3/1	Prepare ad for web	Owner	Prepared a rough draft
			business
2/1-6/1	Place minimum 3-ads/month	Owner & Ad consultant	
	in the print media business		
	& RE Magazines		
3/1-5/1	Prepare circulars and	Owner & WP	
	flyers to do mass Mailings		
5/1-7/1	Put ads in card deck	Jeffrey Lant Owner & their consultant	
6/1-8/15	Acquire Admax website program	Owner & Partners/ Sponsor	completed 10/10/97
6/15-8/30	Receive and prepare		materials to Owner Completed
10/20/97	Send out - tapes and disks		
7/13-9/27	Prepare mailing lists to 5,000	Owner	500 mailing completed
	Use existing list + ad responses	Owner	Send 1000@wk tape
Request			
7/13/-9-27	Update computer skills	Pam/ Sheila DZ Promotions	Completed Internet class &
			adv net ads, web pages,
		training	
10/27-11/3	Send out staggered mailings weekly		

You Are the Architect—Design Your Real Estate Dream

Real Estate Plan

Now let's determine three things that will put you on the right track toward your new business:

1) Who are you?
2) Where are you right now?
3) Where do you want to be?

Hopefully, you have already answered these questions. If so, you will be off to a good start in building a foundation, and can set your eye on the prize—a viable, profitable, Real Estate Investment Business.

By now, you should know the answers that will prompt you to develop your plan. For instance:

▼ How will your business be financed, and for how long?
▼ Who is supporting you?
▼ How will you find your niche market?
▼ Is there a successful person in the Real Estate Investment
▼ Business that you have a relationship with?
▼ Who are your allies; your competition?

Now, you should set a plan of action and challenge yourself to begin the process of embarking on your new business as a Real Estate Investor. So, let's put those final rungs on your ladder toward success. The difference between success and failure is in the planning. No plan, no success. No money.

Think About It

Coming up with, and answering all possible questions, will leave no doubt in what you're trying to accomplish through your Real Estate Investment Business. Finding out as much as possible on a personal level, on a business level, will help you in the beginning, and over the long haul.

Life has no limitations, except the ones you make.
—Les Brown

Chapter 9
"GUTS" Get Up and Tackle Something

During one of the first real estate investment courses that I ever attended, the question was asked, "What is the one characteristic a person needs to do this business?" People guessed everything from money to education, from contacts to experience. The answer was, "<u>GUTS</u>!" I have since used this word to mean: <u>G</u>et <u>U</u>p and <u>T</u>ackle <u>S</u>omething. You've come this far; don't stop now!

Oddly enough, many African-Americans fail to prosper because they've failed to ask themselves "Where am I at now?" or "Where do I want to be in the future?" They often make the process of answering these questions far too complicated. Believe it or not, the simplest way to find out the answers is by taking simple a self-assessment test.

There have been several self-assessment tests throughout this guide. Their primary purpose is to point you in a direction that will help you get started in the Real Estate Investment Business. In the end, you will have to determine your final destination.

Just a Thought...

If you want to go on a trip, you must know your destination, or you'll never get there.

What I've discovered is no matter what the subject, tests are all based on one simple format: A series of questions. So, that tells me *the answers are inside of us.* Think about it. We all have a "little voice"

89

inside of us—our intuition. Some call it their "infinite intelligence" or "inner child". Others call it the "source", "maker", or a "higher power". Whatever the name you give your "little voice", it can be a wealth of guidance.

So, why do you need to take a self-assessment test? You need this test because you need to be clear on the "what" and "why". Although, there have been volumes and volumes written on the subject, as well as hundreds of self-assessment instruments on the market, I promise to keep it simple.

Remember, all tests are based on personal questions. The **key** is you must answer these questions **honestly** and in **writing**. Be sure to complete all the assessments in the journal that you have already started, and that you can continually use. Now, let's begin your Self-Assessment Test by filling in the blanks, as appropriate.

The WHAT Questions

What do I want most in **Life**?
I want _____

What do I want most in a **Job**?
I want _____

What do I want most in a **Relationship**?
I Want _____

What do I want most in a **Business**?
I want _____

What do I want most in a **Marriage**?
I want _____

What do I want most to earn in **Income**?
How much exactly?_____

What do I want most to do in the area of **Investments?**

I want_____

What do I want most to give back to the **World?**

I want_____

Tony Robbins, author of *"Personal Power"* says, "The reason most people don't reach their goals is because they don't have a strong enough *WHY.*" The "why", whether it is fueled by the carrot or the stick, is what *PROPELS* you into action.

This next step of your assessment will incorporate the answers you filled in for **The WHAT Questions** above. Give reasons for the following:

The REASONS Why

Why do I want _____ most in **Life?**

   Because _____

Why do I want _____most in a **Job?**

   Because _____

Why do I want_____ most in a **Relationship?**

   Because _____

Why do I want_____ most in a **Business?**

   Because _____

Why do I want_____ most in a **Marriage?**

   Because _____

Why do I want to make_____ in **Income?**

Because _____

Why do I want _____ the area of **Investments?**

Because _____

Why do I want to give back_____ to the **World** ?

Because _____

In the next set of statements, you will answer **specifically** what you have already accomplished toward the answers in **The WHAT Questions** list.

The FOUNDATION Questions

What have I already built?

As of Today's Date __/__/ __ I have accomplished the following:

What I want most in **Life**

    I have already _____

What I want most in a **Job**

    I have already _____

What I want most in a **Relationship**

    I have already _____

What I want most in a **Business**

    I have already _____

What I want most in a **Marriage**

    I have already _____

What I want most in the area of earning an **Income**

     I have _____

What I want most in the area of **Investments**?

     I have _____

What I want most in giving back to the **World**

     I have _____

In the next set of statements, you will answer **specifically** how you will attain the answers in **The WHAT Questions** list.

The STRATEGY Questions
How will I attain?

What I want most in **Life**.

     I'll do_____

What I want most in a **Job**?

     I'll do_____

What I want most in a **Relationship**?

     I'll do_____

What I want most in a **Business**?

     I'll do_____

What I want most in a **Marriage**?

     I'll do_____

What I want to earn in **Income**?

     I'll do_____

What I want in the area of **Investments**?

     I'll do_____

What I want to give back to the world?

     I'll do_____

Think About It!

Failing To Plan Is a Planning To Fail!

"Believe in God first and then believe in yourself.
There will be nothing the two of you can't achieve."
—Cathy Hughes

Chapter 10
Know Who You Are—Idea Person, Implementer or Maintainer?

Many people are in employment situations that don't match their personality types. Some find themselves bored with their nine-to-five; or, they may see better ways of handling a project, but are not in a position to do anything about it. Some feel totally trapped. Others love their jobs. But for those of you who aren't satisfied, you're probably asking yourself, "What's wrong with me? Why am I so unhappy here?"

It has been said that one of the most important steps to grow either emotionally, financially or spiritually is to know your likes and dislikes, your strengths and weaknesses, your skills, morals, habits, and most importantly, your personality (who you are). We all know that different people have different mindsets, skills and talents and they exhibit them in their own unique way. By now, you are probably asking yourself, "What does all of this have to do with the Real Estate Investing Business?"

To be successful in life, you must walk to the beat of your own drum. Before you decide to start your own Real Estate Investment Business, you need to clearly find out who you are, know what role you are to play in the Real Estate Investment Business, and discover who your friends should be.

Let's discuss "The Three Amigos". They are your three friends, better known as your three personality types, which, I believe relate to your work styles and methods. There isn't a good or bad type; just different approaches to the same scenarios. The purpose for describing these three different personality types is to help you know who you are, how you work, and how you will utilize the resources you need to effectively operate your business to MAKE MORE MONEY.

Take Action!

Before you decide to start your own Real Estate Investment Business, you need to clearly define who you are.

Now let me explain how these totally different personality types function, interact, and work together as it relates to the real estate investment business. Pay close attention to how you interact with people, and how they respond to you.

"IDEA PEOPLE"

The "Idea People" are generally not the ones our society likes to groom. That's why many Idea People seem a little bit out of step; they seem a little bit eccentric. Idea people see a wonderful concept and how well it can be for humanity and mankind. Of the three personality types, Idea People tend to be the highest-paid. They also are usually high risk-takers and could care less what people think. They're used to people saying things like, "I think she's just a little crazy."

Research shows that millionaires (Idea People) gain and lose fortunes an average of three times in their lives. I believe this happens for two reasons:

1) Money is not the most important goal for most millionaires; and

2) It is more important for idea people to get their dreams fulfilled, rather than just earning the money.

However, their road to success only comes true when they surround themselves with good implementers and maintainers. If you're an Idea Person, you will definitely need implementers and maintainers.

People that possess this type of personality tend to be conceptual thinkers and trendsetters. They have foresight and are often visionaries.

"IMPLEMENTERS"

These people can see the "Idea Person's" dreams and/or ideas and make them a reality. They have the ability to design the plans and put together the pieces. Implementers have a unique ability to see the situation from the top; that is, the conceptual level, as well as from the bottom, the maintenance level.

The "Implementers" are the people in between. I call them the swing people—they can function either way. In other words, at times, "Implementers" can be "Idea People"; other times they are "Maintainers". It depends on what's necessary at any given time.

To me, Implementers are the CEOs. They can see the dream or the idea, and have a workable method for getting the idea off the ground and into reality. However, "Implementers" seem to burn out a lot. One reason is because it is very difficult at times to do that balancing act between the "Idea People" and the "Maintainers".

"MAINTAINERS"

Commonly known as the "nine-to-fiver's", these people make up 80 percent of the population, The "Maintainers" are those who make the world go around. They keep the day-to-day operations flowing. They tend to be more interested in one particular part of the whole. It is perfectly logical that there are more maintainers than any other personality type, since once a system is in place, it generally takes more people to keep it running.

"Maintainers" offer stability to any business or organization. They are usually very good at what they do, since they do it over and over again, until it is perfected. Generally, both "Idea People" and "Implementers" need "Maintainers".

How Your Personality Type Will Get Along in the Real Estate Investment Business

Think of a ship. The stern points the ship in the right direction ("Idea People"). The rudder guides the ship and keeps it on course ("Implementers"). Finally, the anchor keeps the ship in place once it reaches its destination ("Maintainers").

I'm an "Idea" person. I am also, of course, in the Real Estate Investment Business. I have to work with people that know what I need and are willing (because they love what they do) to help me get it. For example, my assistant knows what I'm talking about and what to do when I tell her what I need. She knows when and where I need to be and who I need to call. She knows where the paperwork is and she has it ready for me to look over, or to sign, etc. She's like Radar. She's my "Maintainer".

The same is true of my real estate agent. I call her "my jewel". She can pretty much look at a property and know whether or not I would want to buy it—and can make a good offer on it. She can represent me and tell me what I need to do—the pros and cons. I don't have to worry about making a bad investment. She points me in the right direction and gets the ball rolling. She's my "Implementer".

To sum it up, Idea People are traditionally more risk-taking and a little bit more eccentric than other people. Their ideas are unique, and they require someone with a little more foresight—an Implementer—who can see how to earn money using the idea. They usually are not very good at maintaining. Whatever type you are, you need the other two types to make it work.

So, what personality type are you? Look back over your life. What have you done? How did you do it? What are you doing now? Compare the three personality types. Where would you fit in if you where in the Real Estate Investment Business?

Remember!

To enhance your success, you must develop solid business relationships in the world of real estate.

There are several people involved in putting together a real estate transaction; and the other side of knowing your "personality type" is to know the personalities of others in the Real Estate Investment Business. And, more often than not, you may have to adapt the personalities of all "Three Amigos" when you are involved in a real estate transaction. Sometimes at the same time, you may have to deal with buyers, sellers, attorneys, realtors, mortgage brokers, appraisers, code enforcers, and contractors (just to name a few). Real Estate is definitely a people business.

Do Your Homework!

There are many facets to the Real Estate Investment Business. You must find that area of interest that suits you. Define it! Pursue it!

Obviously, since each person has his or her own personality and temperament, at times it becomes a real balancing act to keep a deal together.

Some people are primarily "visual", meaning, they prefer learning by reading information. Other people are "auditory", meaning, they prefer learning through listening methods such audiotapes or CDs.

Finally, some people prefer learning through "kinesthetic methods", for example, interacting with a computer program .

What's amazing is, if you listen, you can hear through people's speech what category they are more likely to be. For example, "I see what you mean (visual)", "I hear what you're saying (auditory)", "I feel like that's true (kinesthetic)". Identifying these qualities, in your Real Estate world of people, can help you steer a deal in the right direction—money!

Knowing What You Do Best will Keep You Focused

As I said earlier, you must know what you like and what you don't like. You need to identify your own personal Real Estate Investment area of interest. It could be wholesale, retail, or rehab, etc. Whatever is on the top of your list, this is what you are going to do best—nothing else will satisfy you.

I cannot stress enough that you need to find out what it is that you like about the Real Estate Investment Business, and once you have found your niche, take your energy and your time, and go full force in that direction.

Think About It!

The difference between success and failure in the Real Estate Investment Business is that it all boils down to being able to maintain a good chemistry when working with a client.

"Today one is held back only by the limits of his or her capabilities and not by man-made blocks and strings."
—Janet Harmon Bragg

Chapter 11

Utilizing your Characteristics, Habits, Traits—to Build Wealth

This chapter is designed to help you recognize the clues that define the character of a person who has succeeded in obtaining undefined wealth.

You may find that many of these clues go as far back as childhood. Perhaps the same characteristics are prevalent in someone you know… it could be one of your children….or. perhaps, it's you.

Just a Thought!

When we look in a mirror, there are three reflections that we see: the child of our past, the person we are today, and the person we will become. With the right role models and the right attitude, we can CHANGE any negative perceptions that have twisted and colored the image of who we really are.

After researching the background of a number of highly successful African-Americans, I learned that all exhibited these four characteristics:

1) Vision (dream)

2) Perseverance (It took several years to build their careers and wealth.)

3) Risk-taking (i.e. calculated risks).

4) Self-management (self-discipline of their time, money and emotions—perfectionists)

In addition, they all tend to have good social skills. They truly love and respect other people. They have great charisma, and give a lot of themselves to their personal causes.

Finally, when I inquired about their definition of success, each touched on the importance of good health, happiness, a good family life, and integrity in their work, etc. What it boils down to is a healthy mental attitude.

Take Note!

An "I'm positive" or "I can" attitude generates the power, skill, and energy needed to do all things. When you believe "I can do it", the "how to do it" develops.

If it is true that success leaves clues, there should be some underlying themes in all successful people. Based on their characteristics, here are some seemingly obvious traits that should be inherent in you, so that you can more easily reach your goal as a successful real estate investor:

▼ You must be clear and focused about what you want, and where you are going in life in order to be successful.

▼ You must be tenacious—never giving up!

▼ You must be encouraged and supported by someone, or something.

▼ You must possess self-discipline, self-management, and most of all, people skills.

Seven Habits of Successful Real Estate Investors

Research shows that there are at least seven habits common to successful real estate investors:

1. Successful Real Estate Investors **Know where they're heading**. The clearer and the more defined the goal, the greater the success.

2. Successful Real Estate Investors **Go into debt only to buy things that will go up in value.** In real estate there is a concept called "highest and best use". It simply means that a piece of land will generate the most income when taken to its highest and best use. For example, a piece of commercial property may have a storefront on it when the highest and best use may be for a hi-rise office building. Or, a piece of beachfront property may have a small house on it when the highest and best use may be for a resort hotel property. *Pay cash for things that go down in value.*

3. Successful Real Estate Investors **Do not Over-Diversify.** When you spread yourself and your resources too thin, a) you cannot make a major impact and, b) you lose focus.

4. Successful Real Estate Investors **Take Reasonable Risks.** There has never been a fortune made without someone taking a calculated risk. This is also where education comes in. If you're going to be a successful real estate investor, you must learn the rules and get the knowledge necessary to procure good deals; thus enabling you to take calculated risks. You can do this by reading, or by participating in seminars and working with mentors.

5. Successful Real Estate Investors **Use Other People's Money (OPM) and Other People's Experience (OPE).** When you are just starting, you can work with a partner; you can get bank financing; you can use seller financing; you can use sweat equity, or whatever else it takes to leverage your time

and money. Leveraging your resources is one of the best methods to gaining wealth.

6. Successful Real Estate Investors **Stay the Course**. This habit has to do with being persistent. Many real estate investors give up just before they reach success. To do anything well you have to have persistence; you have to be willing to stay the course.

   Years one and two are what you call the beginning years. Years three through six are probably the toughest years to go through, a time when many real estate investors give up. When they own several properties and have to deal with management, rentals, taxes, and insurance, it can get most complicated.

   Therefore this is when many real estate investors sell their property. Yet, it is during years seven to ten that you will began to see the first fruits of your labor in the real estate investment market.

7. Successful Real Estate Investors **Take Action**. There's a saying in real estate "If you want to make a lot of money, see a lot of houses and make a lot of offers." The only way you can make money in real estate is either by selling or by controlling a piece of property.

   It is a well-known fact that the people who do the best in business are those who take action. Magical things seem to happen when you *take action*. Very few people are willing to take consistent action. Therefore very few people are independently wealthy.

(Source: *7 Habits of Successful Real Estate Investors* Tape by John Adams. Free subscription to monthly newspaper, order online at www.money99.com)

Take Note!

You must be willing to take some calculated risks in order to gain wealth and success. Part of taking risks means learning and educating yourself in a particular area and becoming an expert.

Six Personal Traits of a Successful Real Estate Investor

"Networking Guru and entrepreneur George C. Fraser (Author, *Success Runs in Our Race*) says that there are at least six common traits inherent in millionaires—Commitment, Uniqueness, Toughness, Willingness to Learn, Courage, and Unwillingness to Fail. He suggests a self assessment to see if you possess any of these traits.

What Are You Committed To?

People don't try any of the stuff that they read about in magazines unless they are committed to their work. There's a skill to understanding what people are really committed to, as opposed to what they think they're committed to.

▼ What exactly are you willing to risk for that commitment?

▼ Are you more committed to the friends you make in business school than you are to your business plan?

▼ If it came right down to it, would you sell those guys out if you thought that they might be going in a different direction than you?

At the end of the day, you have to do a forced ranking of your commitments.

What Mark Are You Trying To Make?

Even more important is the question "On behalf of what are you trying to make your mark?" I ask that a lot, and it startles people. They don't want to say, "On behalf of my ego. I want to be a big shot. I want some publicity. I want to be a big deal." Actually, those are all okay answers. But I want to know the real answer. So when people talk about making their mark, I say, "Great!"

Write down your answers in your journal:

- ▼ What mark do you want to make?
- ▼ What would it look like?
- ▼ What would it be on behalf of?"

And I want really thoughtful answers to those questions. I don't care as much about the content of the answer as I do about the authenticity of it.

Are You Tough Enough?

A successful Real Estate Investor needs to have an emotional maturity and toughness. Any hard project is guaranteed to stir up a wide range of emotions. Take, for example, running out of money just when your team needs you to keep the faith.

On the one hand, you're scared to death. On the other hand, you have to keep a stiff upper lip. I also look for a balance of optimism and grounded reality.

Optimism, without grounded reality, is a dream. Grounded reality, without optimism, is boring. People who are emotionally tough are always saying, "There's got to be a way." Business is not life threatening; it's ego threatening. And the people who are willing to risk their ego are emotionally tough.

Are You a Learning Machine?

To succeed as a real estate investor, you have to be a learning machine. You have to let the environment and your team inform you. At the same time, you also need to have a balance between being open to ideas and pushing forward in the face of skepticism.

There's one extreme, where lots of people offer lots of different opinions, and the leader winds up utterly confused about what to do next. Then there's the other extreme, where Real Estate Investors think that they know it all, and don't allow themselves to be informed and corrected. To succeed, you must have a strong vision but allow that vision to be affected by other great points of view.

Are You Courageous?

Do you have the courage to change course, to stay committed to the outcome, and to do things differently than you anticipated doing them? Are you courageous enough to change the whole plan if you find a better way?

Are you Unwilling to Fail?

There's a lot of lore around the words "failure is not an option." That's just a cute phrase.

The meaningful way to think about it is, "We said that we were going to make this work, damn it, so how?" When leaders acknowledge failure, they drag a lot of attention away from the "how."

FYI—There's No Such Thing as Failure!

Most successful Real Estate Investors believe failure is so uninteresting to them that they don't really care if it's pretty or ugly. Their idea is, "We're going to make it. And we're going to focus on the how. The road's blocked? Let's find another one."

I believe that if you have acquired any of these valuable traits, it can mean the difference between owning a successful Real Estate Investment Business or just having an interesting idea that goes nowhere.

Believe You Can Succeed and You Will

▼ Here are some mindsets of success that you can take to heart.

▼ The "how to do it" always comes to the person who believes he or she can do it.

▼ Strong belief triggers the mind to figure the ways and means.

▼ Belief in success is absolutely the most essential ingredient for success.

▼ The "Okay, I'll give it a try, but I don't think it will work" attitude produces failure.

Disbelief is negative power. When the mind disbelieves or doubts, the mind attracts "reasons" to support the disbelief. Doubt, disbelief, a subconscious will to fail, or a "not really wanting to succeed" attitude is responsible for most failures.

▼ Think doubt, and fail. Think victory, and succeed.
▼ Believe in yourself and good things will start happening.
▼ Success isn't based on luck.
▼ The size of your success is determined by the size of your belief.

Success arrives over time and is based upon belief in yourself, your abilities, and your worth.

With a strong and healthy belief in yourself, you can go out and survive the stress of day-to-day living and reach worthy goals. You are always valuable and your actions are learning experiences; not to be repeated, if negative, but to be reinforced constantly, if positive.

▼ We are what we see, what we do, and most importantly WHAT WE THINK.

▼ Successful people make life happen FOR THEM— NOT TO THEM.

▼ Success is the journey, not the destination.

▼ The only difference between stumbling blocks and stepping-stones is the way we use them.

How well you are doing is not the main issue; it's whether you perceive that you are doing well that counts.

Think About It!

Think success. Don't think failure. Thinking success conditions your mind to create plans that produce success. Thinking failure does the exact opposite. **Successful people seek a solution in every problem, rather than a problem in every solution.**

I can accept failure. Everyone fails at something.
But I can't accept not trying
—Michael Jordan

Chapter 12

Get Ready! Get Set!
It's Time To Get Started!

Start where you are, with what you've got, doing whatever you can, NOW. In order to start from where you are, the most important point, again, is to know yourself. I keep going back to that point because it is extremely critical.

You must know yourself in order to identify those skills that you have, especially ones that are **transferable** to a Real Estate Investment Business. You must look into your repertoire and find out what they are.

In fact, there are activities that you are performing right now that will help you in making the transition to your Real Estate Investment Business. See which transferable skills you already have.

1. Do you have Organization skills?

2. Do you have Problem-solving skills?

3. Do you have Research skills (can you find things on the net, in the phone guide, in the newspapers)?

4. Are you a good observer?

5. Are you a good motivator (can you get people to do things, give you information)?

6. Are you good at being persistent and following up?

7. Do you have any managerial skills (have you ever coached a team, or have you ever coordinated a charity function)?

8. Are you a mother running a household and working?

9. Are you a single parent?

10. Have you ever chaired a committee or group, at your church, school or work?

If you answered YES to one or more questions above, you have some transferable skills to be used in the Real Estate Investment Business. Here are some other points to consider:

▼ Are you curious?

▼ Do you communicate well with people? Do you show genuine concern?

▼ Do you have a good imagination?

▼ Do you like challenges?

▼ Will you take "No!" for an answer?

▼ Do you enjoy helping people solve problems?

▼ Do you listen well? (This, by the way, is key)

▼ Are you flexible in your thinking?

Take Note!

None of these questions or points deal with finance, numbers, analysis or even real estate. But they do deal with some skills you already bring to the table that can help you develop your Real Estate Investment Business.

For example, I had a transferable skill in administration, a field, I worked in for fourteen years, and in which I received my graduate degree. Administration taught me how to do all the things necessary to run a business day-to-day, such as coordinating activities, locating resources, managing staff, etc.

Administration also taught me problem resolution, which is a good asset to have. If you want to make a lot of money, you must learn to focus on problem resolution, not problem description. Many of us can tell the what, when, who, and why, but we end up dwelling on the problem, not the solution. That focus needs to be turned around and all your time, energy, and money, should be spent on *PROBLEM SOLVING.*

It takes several components to pull a real estate deal together, therefore you are going to have to have the skills to work with all of types of people at the same time.

Another transferable skill I had was in research. While selling real estate in Georgia, I conducted a social market research in the Atlanta Metro area and surrounding counties, such as Fulton, Dekalb, Cobb and Gwinnet. One of the skills required was the ability to locate families.

This was a longitudinal study that covered a 10-year period. We had to interview a number of people the first year; then the same people again in years three and four. Then, after 10 years, we had to interview the same people again.

The types of people that were part of the study were not the most stable, and did not always stay in one place very long. Therefore my job also required some detective work to locate these people.

Oftentimes, when you see a vacant, boarded up house that has been sitting two or three years (which many times will turn out to be a very good deal), your biggest task will be to find the owner. If it were very simple to locate those owners, everyone would be doing it. Therefore, you're going to have to use skills that other people do not have, nor will take the time to develop.

Having already developed those skills set me apart, and allowed me to make deals that other people weren't able to make. Now let's take a closer look to see if your transferable skills can help you start your Real Estate Investment Business, NOW!

The Self-Employment Test, unlike most tests, is meant to be confidence building. *There are no right or wrong answers.*

Once you know your assets (and liabilities), and as long as you are always willing to learn new skills, and surround yourself with the right people, who can provide the skills you lack, you can be a successful Real Estate Investor.

Before you step out there, let's take one more look into your background. Once you ask yourself the following questions, you'll be able to figure out your score and then, based on your score you'll learn more about your potential to become a successful Real Estate Investor. Use this exercise to help you get on, or stay on course.

Please answer the following questions YES or NO

1. Do you want to go into business for yourself?_____

2. When you look in the mirror, do you see an entrepreneur?_____

3. Is your decision to go into business for yourself one of action, or reaction?_____

4. Are you afraid of failing or succeeding?_____

5. Do you have staying power?_____

6. Would you consider yourself confident?_____

7. Can you take control of your life?_____

8. Could you hire or fire someone?_____

9. Are you comfortable working with others?_____

10. Are you creative?_____

11. Would you consider yourself passionate?_____

12. Are you afraid of taking risks?_____

13. Do you know the difference between a risk and a gamble?_____

14. Did you want to own a business when you grew up?_____

15. Do you have the ability to set goals?_____

16. Do you have a track record for achieving goals?_____

17. Are you in good health?_____

18. Do you have a high energy level?_____

19. Are you intimidated by lawyers, accountants, bankers, the IRS? _____

20. Can you give up the security of a regular paycheck?_____

21. Can you write clearly?_____

22. Are you afraid of speaking in public?_____

23. Do you have the ability to listen?_____

24. Do you enjoy selling?_____

25. Can you distinguish between a setback and a defeat?_____

26. Can you honestly assess your strengths and your weaknesses? _____

27. Would you characterize yourself as decisive?_____

28. Would you characterize yourself as organized?_____

29. Would you characterize yourself as a day dreamer?_____

30. Does your family support you decision to go into business for yourself?_____

Let's Recap!

If you answered yes to:

1-19 Questions—**Wait awhile before you go into business.** Based on your self-employment score, you're not sure if you really want to be self-employed at this time. You should wait until you're absolutely sure.

20-24 Questions—**Start slowly… maybe part-time at first.** Your self-employment entrepreneurial skills are encouraging, but you should start off very slow perhaps part-time at first. In time, your self-employment skills could improve, making you a great future prospects for self-employment in the future.

25-39 Questions—**Start now. You're ready.** Your self-employment intuition is high, and based on the usual entrepreneurial principles, would give you an above average chance for success.

The following are broader descriptions, based on your answers to the preceding exercise. They are derived from a compilation of information representing various resources, including my experience in operating my own Real Estate Investment Business for several years.

1: Do you really want to start your own Real Estate Investment Business?

Starting your own Real Estate Investment Business is a good decision. However, you must also believe that you can provide the best product or service in your industry. You must also know that you have the skills, the stamina, and the guts to stay the course long enough for your business to prosper.

2: Who do you see when you look in the mirror?

In other words, do you like yourself? Sometimes, going into business for yourself is a lonely journey. You must have positive self-esteem because you may not have anyone cheering you on. Also, you may not have the luxury of a paycheck every week.

Your clients—the people that you will serve—are in essence counting on what you bring to the table as their paycheck.

It will be highly unlikely that you will succeed if you don't like yourself and have no self-confidence in your abilities.

3: Is your decision to embark into a real estate investment business, one of action, or reaction?

Is your job not fulfilling enough? Is starting a real estate investment business an ambition of your spouse? Did you decide that this is the only way you could put your kids through college? These may all be good reasons to proceed, but make sure you are not just trying to avoid certain situations rather than moving toward a positive goal of your choice—which may not be to start your own business.

4: Are you afraid of failing and/or succeeding?

Fear of failure and fear of success are two sides of the same coin. They suffer from the "glass is half full/glass is half empty syndrome". The optimist looks at a glass of water and says the glass is half full. The pessimist looks at the glass of water and says the glass is half empty.

However, someone who starts a business has to conquer both the fear of failure, and the fear of success. Make the glass **full**. If you don't overcome fear, you will sabotage your success. The key is to look at success from a standpoint that you "worked for it and you deserve it!"

5: Do you have staying power?

It has often been said that many people give up just as they are on the verge of success—just before they make that long-awaited breakthrough. Throughout this guide, you have learned ways to maintain the stamina, persistence, and "staying power" needed in order to become a successful real estate investor.

6: Do you think of yourself as confident?

Confidence is a characteristic that separates champions from the ordinary; the winners from the losers; the rich from the poor. Confidence is that unshakable knowledge that you know whatever you conceive, if you believe, you can achieve!

7: Do you have control over your life?

One of the primary reasons people want to start a business is so they can have control over their lives. However, the primary component of self-control is self-discipline. You must maintain control over your most precious commodity—your time.

When you are in your own business, the challenge is to do only those tasks that earn you the highest hourly rate and allow you to delegate the rest.

8: Can you successfully hire or fire someone?

Hiring and firing your team members is always a judgment call. It is an absolute, but crucial judgment call when it's your own business. This decision, like any other, should be based upon good information. You've got to do your homework.

There is an additional element: Compatibility. When you're hiring for your real estate investment business, keep in mind that a potential team member can be the best capable, but if he or she is not compatible, you will lose precious time attempting to work out personality issues, instead of your business. You should always take the time to develop personality compatibility tests.

9: Are you completely comfortable working with others?

Studies show that successful business people are oftentimes loners. This can be both a positive and a negative. Sometimes it is best that you handle things yourself. On the other hand, you cannot build or administer a real estate business alone. So be sure that your reason for going into a real estate investment business is to move toward providing a good product or service; not just running away from a bad situation, such as a job, because "I can do it by myself".

10: Do You consider yourself creative?

Creativity in business is different than that what most people think… such as, coming up with a great concept. It means being dynamic; keeping it moving; growing in success.

11: Do you consider yourself a passionate person?

You need passion to sustain your business; it's crucial. It helps you to get up in the morning and the day after. Your passion is what will help you come up with other ways to market your real estate investment business and find new clients. That passion is what will help you strive towards success, even during seemingly failing periods. Without *fat-burning* passion, your real estate investment business will whither and die.

12: Are you afraid of taking risks?

This is another defining characteristic of super successful people. Many people are only too willing to go through life playing it safe. You can't make a run to second base, while keeping your foot on first base. It cannot be done. By definition, real estate investors must be comfortable with a certain amount of risk-taking. Being in business is not for the faint of heart. You must be willing to move out of your comfort zone.

13: Do you know the difference between a calculated risk and a gamble?

To be a successful real estate investor, you must respect the difference between gambling, and calculated risk-taking. A calculated risk is based upon objective data and complete information. You must do your homework. Gambling, on the other hand, is based upon incomplete and unsubstantiated information. If you are undisciplined and inclined toward gambling, you need to stay away from real estate investing.

14: When you were a child, what did you want to be when you grew up?

What did you enjoy doing? Did you make money babysitting? Did you have a newspaper route? A lemonade stand? Did you walk dogs or cut lawns for your neighbors? These are all forms of entrepreneurship.

Studies indicate that many people who exhibited entrepreneurship tendencies early in life became successful business leaders. However, it isn't an exact science.

15: Do you have the ability to set goals?

Unfortunately, the answer to this question is non-negotiable if you want to be a successful real estate investor. As the head of your business, you must be able to set goals, and be creative enough to figure out how to carry them out on behalf of yourself, your clients and your professional team.

16: Do you have a track record for accomplishing your goals?

A simple way to answer this question is to look back over the past year and ask yourself if you accomplished what you set out to do at the beginning of the year. In other words, did you stay in your comfort zone? You've heard the old adage, "Show me a person that has not failed, and I'll show you a person that has not attempted to do anything."

17: How's your health?

Most companies still require employees to take a physical examination; particularly if they offer medical benefits. As the owner of your own real estate investment business, you are likely to be under more stress, work longer hours, eat irregularly, and/or not get enough sleep. So when you start your real estate investment business, you should take a physical exam and get a good stamp of approval on your health. If you are not in good health, you could be a disaster waiting to happen.

18: Do you have a high level of energy?

You need high levels of energy to keep others energized around you (i.e. your team, clients, outside professionals). High energy levels and self-confidence usually go hand-in-hand.

19: Are you intimidated by lawyers, accountants, bankers, the IRS, or other authority figures?

This question is for all who are intimidated by authority figures. Think about it. What do all of these people have in common? They are all paid employees in some form or another; oftentimes paid to work for companies and corporations. They are also in a service business and they want to have satisfied customers and clients just like you.

Find people that are assets (not liabilities) to you. This means being able to build trust and rapport. Yes, this can be accomplished even with the toughest "authority" figures.

20: Can you give up the security of a regular paycheck?

This is another key component to having your own real estate investment business. For most of us, security is receiving a regular paycheck each pay period. If we do the job, we expect a check. The security of a paycheck allows us to plan and live very effectively.

Some of you, when beginning a new business venture, will either have to do it part-time, and keep the security of a paycheck, or you will have to have enough money set aside to cover those expenses that come—paycheck or not. Either way, there is a period of uncertainty.

Can you live with that uncertainty? Can your family? There's a cost/benefit effect. If you keep your job, in order to keep a pay check, and run your business part-time, you will have to be in good health, and your family will have to be okay with seeing you less. However, it will take longer to accomplish your goals. In other words, it's a trade off.

21: Can you effectively communicate in writing?

You will have to be able to effectively express yourself in written form. You must be able to write clear contracts, and marketing materials, etc. If necessary, you can hire a good assistant to do a great portion of your correspondence. But initially, you may not be able to afford one. Until then, every correspondence, contract and/or marketing piece must come from you, and it must be understood by the reader.

22: Can you speak in public?

Public speaking seems to be the number one fear for most people. Depending upon the focus of your Real Estate Investment Business, you may not have to speak to large crowds. You will, however, have to address different types of "crowds" like your clients, your own group of professionals, and your competitors. In doing so, you must especially be able to explain your business in detail.

23: Do you consider yourself a good listener?

This is another key component. Believe it or not, listening is an art form. Those who master it, get paid handsomely. Why? Because they can hear what their client is really saying. By being an effective listener, you can construct effective solutions. Everybody wins!

24: Do you like selling?

The truth of the matter is, we are always selling something - ourselves, or our ideas. As a real estate investor, you will be selling your product or service. However, you will do it in your own style; using your passion and enthusiasm. Some selling methods call for the ability to persuade, negotiate, and/or posture. If you find the selling process repulsive, then owning a real estate investment business may not be your forte.

25: Do you know the difference between a setback and a defeat?

Losing a bid on a multi-unit building to another real estate investor is a defeat. Having an investor pull his or her money out of a deal two weeks before closing is a setback. In the first situation, there is no way to recover the deal (defeat). However, in the second situation, you have time to save the deal (setback).

26: Can you honestly assess your strengths and your weaknesses?

This is another key component to becoming a successful real estate investor. "Honesty" is the operative word here. Competent people tend to overestimate their abilities and their strengths. Sometimes this is a good thing, because it causes them to take risks. However, sometimes it keeps them from getting the help they need.

All of us have strengths and weaknesses, but identifying them honestly is what counts. For example, you might attempt to maintain the financial books and records yourself, instead of hiring a good accountant. A real estate investor must know what the costs are; what the break-even point is; and, what the profit margin is, in order to stay in business. If mathematics is difficult for you, there's an accountant out there who can do these calculations in his or her sleep. You must evaluate each situation separately, and apply brutal honesty in every case.

27: Do you see yourself as a decision maker?

Would you call yourself decisive? A real estate investor has no choice but to make decisions. Some will be good decisions, others will not. Remember (GUTS) "Get Up And Tackle Something"? That statement characterizes the real estate investor. Also, remember, no decision is a decision. So if you're sitting on the fence, you have made a decision not to move forward.

28: Do you see yourself as organized?

Organization will have to be your mantra. The reason we have spent so much time on self-assessment, is so you can organize your thoughts before you actually begin your new real estate investment business. Any business you start needs organization in order to run successfully.

29: Do you consider yourself a daydreamer?

Being a daydreamer is a positive asset. Daydreaming is what sparks creativity and new ideas, and what provides inspiration. New businesses need constant shots of newness—new methods, new solutions to all problems, and new ways of getting more clients, etc.

30: Does your family support your decision to start your own real estate investment business?

The best way to ensure this support, is to sit down as a family and plan your new endeavor together. Your new real estate investment business will require adjustments emotionally, financially, and physically. As feasible as possible, include (or involve) your family in the "goings-on" of the business.

Think About It!

Owning and running a real estate investment business is a major decision. Make sure that this is not a disguise of another goal and that you have the knowledge and skills to make it work! More importantly, make sure you are moving toward this wonderful impasse in your life, and not putting yourself, or the welfare of your family, into a costly mistake! If you have maintained a passionate "Yes, I can!" you are ready! Congratulations!

Successful African-American
Real Estate Investors...How They Did It!

Monique Greenwood

Monique Greenwood is CEO of Akwaaba Enterprises, Inc., which operates Bed and Breakfast inns in New York, New Jersey and DC, a restaurant, commercial buildings and residential apartments in Bedford Stuyvesant, Brooklyn.

Ms. Greenwood was former editor-in-chief of Essence Magazine, but left the publishing world to run her real estate investment business full time. In 1995, Ms. Greenwood and her husband Glenn Pogue purchased a dilapidated 18-room mansion in Brooklyn, New York, and restored it to an elegant bed- and-breakfast called Akwaaba Mansion.

In 1998, the success of the inn led to a 72-seat restaurant down the street called Akwaaba Café. Later the couple bought a nearby building with 150 building violations, financed the restoration, and rented it at affordable rates to local entrepreneurs seeking to open businesses that would complement the bed and breakfast and café. Monique believes we can reclaim our communities, block by block, and she and her husband Glenn Pogue are doing just that. Their business, Akwaaba Properties owns the block of Lewis Avenue, between MacDonough and Decatur Streets, where they have developed the Shops of Lewis Avenue. Other businesses include Brownstone Books, The Parlor Floor Antiques, Jones Barber Shop, Marlene's Hair Salon and Mirrors Coffee House, which is owned by Monique's ten-year-old daughter Glynn.

The couple has also opened Akwaaba by the Sea in Cape May, New Jersey and Akwaaba D.C., a renovated 1920s brownstone in the Dupont Circle area of Monique's Washington, DC hometown.

A magna cum laude graduate of Howard University and an alumna of the Program for Developing Managers at Simmons Graduate School of Business, Monique is the author of the new book "Having What Matters: The Black Woman's Guide to Creating the Life You Really Want."

Jerline Lambert

Jerline Lambert first began in real estate in 1965, when she went to work as a sales representative for Well's Realty in Chicago. In 1968, she became a real estate broker and opened up Lambert's Realty, serving as president and CEO. She took classes and became the first African American woman certified real estate manager. Since then, her business has grown to include real estate appraisals and property management, incorporating a staff of fifteen, including four of Lambert's children.

In recent years, Lambert was appointed by the National Association of Realtors to work as district coordinator for Illinois Congressman Danny Davis, bringing to his attention various housing related issues throughout his district.

She has also been involved in a number of community organizations and has been the recipient of numerous awards. She was appointed by former Illinois Governor Jim Edgar to serve as a member of the Governor's Commission of Mortgage Practices; is president emeritus of the Chicago Chapter of Africare; and the first vice president of the Midwest Community Council. Lambert has also served on the national board of Operation PUSH and has been the recipient of the Rainbow/PUSH Women in Business Achievement Award.

Jerline Lambert was born in West Helena, Arkansas. She earned a B.A. from Northwestern University in Chicago in 1989. Ms. Lambert also received a variety of other certifications, including a certified real estate appraiser license from Howard University and a certified real estate manager license from the University of Chicago.

Richmond McCoy

Prominent real estate executive Richmond McCoy was born to a large family in 1954 in upstate New York and grew up in a rural area where his parents owned a dairy farm. His father also owned several apartment buildings in Harlem and young Richmond often accompanied him to collect rent, sowing the seeds of his interest in real estate at an early age. When he was a teenager, McCoy's father died unexpectedly, leaving his mother and siblings to fend for themselves. After graduating from high school, McCoy left for the West Coast, where he sold encyclopedias.

After returning to New York and pursuing sales and other opportunities, McCoy decided to pursue a career in commercial real estate, obtaining his license in 1979. In 1984, McCoy embarked on his first entrepreneurial venture when he became one of the founding partners of Richard Sykes & Partners. There, McCoy widened his base of knowledge by doing transactions throughout the United States. In 1991, seeing a possible niche, McCoy set up his own firm, the R.M.C. Group, to provide corporate real estate services to major companies that wanted to work with minority-owned enterprises. By 1993, McCoy's business had expanded and he created the McCoy Realty Group to provide asset management services to pension funds and large financial institutions such as Pitney-Bowes, Chase Manhattan Bank, and the Teachers Insurance and Annuity Association, the world's largest privately managed pension fund.

By the mid-1990s McCoy saw a growing need for real estate and institutional asset management in African American communities and the non-profit sector. He attempted to fulfill these needs with the founding of UrbanAmerica. As president and CEO, McCoy has seen UrbanAmerica grow tremendously. Some of its projects have included shopping malls in Florida, medical offices in Las Vegas and police precincts in Maryland.

Roy Donahue Peebles

Roy Donahue Peebles is recognized as the first African American to truly diversify South Florida's all-white ranks of developers. After a lengthy process, Peebles' company, Peebles Atlantic Development Corporation, was chosen to build the $60 million project.

In 1995, while on vacation in Miami with his wife and young son, Peebles read an article about Miami's search for a black developer to develop two old beach hotels, the Shorecrest and the Royal Palm.

In 1998, Peebles purchased the historic Miami Beach Bath Club that he developed into a luxury condominium complex.

Born on March 2, 1960, the only son of a civil servant and a real estate broker, Roy Donahue Peebles grew up in Washington, D.C. After his parents' divorce in 1967, Peebles moved with his mother to Detroit, spending only six months there before returning to Washington, D.C., to live with his father.

Peebles is the vice chairman of the Greater Miami Conventions and Visitors Bureau, a former board member of Florida International University, and a member of the Visitors Industry Council Board. He resides in Coral Gables, Florida with his wife, Katrina, and their young son, Donahue Peebles III.

As a teenager, Peebles worked as a congressional page and attended the United States Capitol Page High School, where he graduated in 1978. Following high school, he enrolled in Rutgers University, planning to go into medicine. He dropped out after a year and found a job doing real estate appraisals. His career took a meteoric rise after Mayor Marion Barry appointed him, at age twenty-three, to chair the city's property tax board. This job gave him the opportunity and the connections to develop a successful real estate career. He was the first black developer to attempt to build an office building in downtown Washington.

Philip Payton

Philip Payton, whose father was a barber and mother a hairdresser, was born in 1876, in Westfield, Massachusetts. After learning the barber trade, and after an unsuccessful year of study at Livingstone College in Salisbury, North Carolina, Payton headed for New York City, without any certain plans. In New York, he worked as a barber and at various menial jobs, saving what he could. In 1900, he got a job in a real estate office, which paid more than his barbering. It was there that he decided what he wanted to do with his life.

With a partner, he rented a very small, very modest office in Manhattan and opened his first real estate business. It proved a colossal failure, but failure only seemed to whet Payton's appetite to succeed. Payton's customary amount of cash to leave the house with was fifteen cents; five cents to ride downtown, five cents for luncheon and five cents to ride back up town at night. His wife was doing sewing, a day's work or anything else she could get to do to help him along... All his friends discouraged him and tried to convince him that there was no show for a colored man in such a business in New York.

Philip managed to secure another house after a while, and he and his wife moved in. Seemingly, this was the turning point in my business career. Things began to pick up and eventually he bought the flat house in which he was living. Then he bought two more flats and kept them five months until he sold them at a profit of $5,000. He bought another, kept it a month, and made $2,750, another and made $1,500, another and made $2,600, and so on. In a while Payton had held title to $250,000 worth of New York realty.

Soon after, Payton and several other black businessmen formed the Afro-American Realty Company, initially to save a number of buildings on West 135th Street, from which dozens of African-American tenants were to be evicted. Payton and his partners first attempted to lease the particular buildings. When this failed, they bought two of them outright, which effectively put an end to the attempted evictions. The Afro-American Realty Company went on to purchase and develop many other buildings in Harlem, and Payton became respected as a major figure in Harlem realty.

Herman Russell

Born in 1930 in the ghetto of Atlanta, Herman Russell was the youngest of eight children. His father was a plasterer, and young Herman learned the business well. By 12, he was already an accomplished tradesman. At 16, he even purchased a parcel of land for $125 that he and some friends used to build a duplex. Eventually, he enrolled at Tuskegee University, working summers to finish the building project. When completed, rent derived from the two-family structure helped finance his education. After graduating from Tuskegee University, he returned to Atlanta to work alongside his father as a plastering subcontractor. In 1953, the son extended his father's business into general contracting and H.J. Russell & Company was born.

Russell was on his way to becoming a builder of 500-unit complexes and some of our nation's most celebrated skylines bear his imprint. He became full venture partner in such projects as Metro Atlanta Rapid Transit Authority train stations, construction of parking decks at Hartsfield International Airport and the $115 million Georgia Pacific Corporation office tower. H. J. Russell & Company went on to expand into food and communications and employ 1,500 people in 11 subsidiaries with annual sales topping $286 million.

Over the course of his career, Herman Russell has received many awards and honor, including: The Entrepreneur of the Year Lifetime Achievement Award and Dow Jones Entrepreneurial Excellence Award.

Dempsey Travis

In 1949, at the age of 29, Dempsey Travis founded Travis Realty Corporation and became its president. In addition to his responsibilities at Travis Realty, Travis also served as president of Sivart Mortgage Company. At the helm of these two companies, Travis was able to establish himself firmly in the real estate development of Chicago's South Side throughout the latter half of the twentieth century.

In 1960, Travis founded United Mortgage Bankers of America, as well as the Dempsey Travis Securities and Investment Corporation, which he served as president until 1974. Travis received a Bachelor's degree from Roosevelt University and an advanced degree from the School of Mortgage Banking at Northwestern University.

Travis founded the Urban Research Press in 1969 as a forum for the publication of African American literature and nonfiction, which has since published seven best-selling nonfiction books by Travis, as well as those of several other writers. He has also served as president of the Society of Midland Authors, financial editor for Dollars and Sense, and as a contributing writer for *Ebony* and Black Scholar. He was a coordinator of Dr. Martin Luther King, Jr.'s 1960 March on Chicago, president of the NAACP Chicago Chapter from 1959 to 1960 and has participated in several presidential administrations.

Appendix B
African American Resources

African American Banks

Carver Bancorp, Inc.
Deborah Wright, President & CEO
75 West 125th Street
New York, NY 10027
(212)876-4747 | FAX (212)426-6214

Independence Federal Savings Bank
Donna Shuler, President & CEO
1229 Connecticut Avenue, NW
Washington, D.C. 20036
(202)628-5500 | FAX (202)626-7106

Industrial Bank, N.A.
Doyle Mitchell, President & CEO
4812 Georgia Avenue, NW
Washington, DC 20011
(202)722-2000 | FAX (202)722-2040

Highland Community Bank
George Bar, CEO
1701 W. 87th Street
Chicago, IL 60620
(773)881-6800 | FAX (773)881-7567

Seaway National Bank of Chicago
Walter E Grady, President & CEO
645 East 87th Street
Chicago, IL 60619
(773)487-4800 | FAX (773)487-0452

Citizens Trust Bank of Atlanta
James E Young, President & CEO
75 Piedmont Avenue
Atlanta, GA 30303
(404)653-2800 | FAX (404)584-7766

Family Savings Bank, FSB
Wayne-Kent A Bradshaw, President &
CEO
3683 Crenshaw Blvd.
Los Angeles, CA 90016
(213)295-3381 | FAX (213)296-6801

Liberty Bank and Trust Company
Alden J McDonald, CEO
P.O. Box 60131
New Orleans, LA 70160
(504)286-8861 | FAX (504)286-8866

City National Bank of New Jersey
Louis E Prezeau, CEO
900 Broad Street
Newark, NJ 07102
(973)624-0865 | FAX (973)624-4369

The Harbor Bank of Maryland
Joseph Haskins, CEO
25 West Fayette Street
Baltimore, MD 21201
(410)528-1800 | FAX (410)528-1420

Mechanics and Farmers Bank
Lee Johnson, Jr, Chairman, President &
CEO
116 West Parrish Street
Durham, NC 27701
(919)683-1521 | FAX (919)687-7821

Broadway Federal Bank
Paul C Hudson, President & CEO
4835 W. Venice Blvd.
Los Angeles, CA 90019
(213)931-1886 | FAX (213)931-2272

Consolidated Bank and Trust Co.
Vernard W Henley, Chairman
320 North First Street
Richmond, VA 23219
(804)771-5200 | FAX (804)771-5269

Illinois Service Federal S&L Association
Thelma J Smith, President & CEO
4619 South King Drive
Chicago, IL 60653
(773)624-2000 | FAX (773)624-5340

United Bank of Philadelphia
Emma Chappell, Chairman, President & CEO
714 Market Street
Philadelphia, PA 19106
(215)829-2265 | FAX (215)829-2269

Founders National Bank of Los Angeles
John Kelly, President & CEO
3910 W. MLK, Jr. Blvd.
Los Angeles, CA 90008
(213)290-4848 | FAX (213)290-3313

First Independence National Bank
Donald Davis, Chairman
44 Michigan Avenue
Detroit, MI 48226
(313)256-8400 | FAX (313)256-8811

Tri State Bank of Memphis
Jesse H Turner, Chairman & President
180 South Main at Beale
Memphis, TN 38103
(901)525-0384 | FAX (901)526-8608

Citizens Federal Savings Bank
Bunny Stokes, CEO
1700 3rd Avenue North
Birmingham, AL 35203
(205)328-2041 | FAX (205)214-3070

Dryades Savings Bank, FSB
Virgil Robinson, President & CEO
231 Carondelet Street Suite 200
New Orleans, LA 70130
(504)581-5891 | FAX (504)598-7233

OneUnited Bank
Kevin Cohee, Chairman & CEO
133 Federal Street
Boston, MA 02110
1-877-ONE-UNITED
1-877-663-8648

Douglass National Bank
Ronald Wiley, President & CEO
1670 E. 63rd Street
Kansas City, MO 64110
(913)321-7200 | FAX (913)321-7519

Mutual Community Savings Bank Inc., SSB
William G. Smith, President & CEO
315 E. Chapel Hill Street
Durham, NC 27701
(919)688-1308 | FAX (919)682-1380

First Tuskegee Bank
James W Wright, Chairman & CEO
301 North Elm Street
Tuskegee, AL 36083
(334)262-0800 | FAX (334)265-4333

Capitol City Bancshares Inc
George Andrews, President
562 Lee Street S.W.
Atlanta, GA 30310
(404) 752-6067 | FAX (404)752-5862

Consolidated Bank & Trust C.
V. W. Henley, Chairman & CEO
320 North First Street
P.O. Box 26823
Richmond, VA 23261-6823
(804)771-5200 | FAX (804)771-5244

United Bank of Philadelphia
714 Market St.
Philadelphia, PA 19106
215-829-2265

African American Insurance Companies

North Carolina Mutual Life Ins. Co.
Bert Collins, President & CEO
411 West Chapel Hill Street
Durham, NC 27701
(919)682-9201 | FAX (919)683-1694

Atlanta Life Insurance Company
Charles H Cornelius, President & CEO
100 Auburn Avenue N.E.
Herndon Plaza
Atlanta, GA 30303
(404)659-2100 | FAX (404)654-8808

Golden State Mutual Life Insurance Co.
Larkin Teasley, President & CEO
1999 West Adams Blvd.
Los Angeles, CA 90018
(213)731-1131 | FAX (213)732-2139

Gertrude Geddes Willis Life Insurance
Co.
Joseph Misshore Jr., President & CEO
2120 Jackson Avenue
New Orleans, LA 70113
(504)522-2525 | FAX (504)522-2805

Booker T. Washington Insurance Co.
Kirkwood R Balton, Chairman,
President & CEO
1728 3rd Avenue, North
Birmingham, AL 35203
(205)328-5454 | FAX (205)251-6873

Protective Industrial Insurance Co.
James C Harrison, President & CEO
2300 11th Avenue North
Birmingham, AL 35234
(205)323-5256 | FAX (205)251-7614

Winnfield Life Insurance Company
Charles Henderson, President
315 North Street
Natchitoches, LA 71457
(318)352-8346 | FAX (318)352-8722

Williams-Progressive Life & Acc. Ins. Co
Patrick Fontenot, President
348 South Academy Street
Opelousas, LA 70570
(318)948-8238 | FAX (318)948-2099

Golden Circle Life Insurance Co.
Cynthia Rawls Bond, President
39 South Jackson Ave.
Brownsville, TN 38012
(901)772-9283 | FAX (901)772-9285

Reliable Life Insurance Company
Joseph H Miller, CEO
718 Jackson St.
Monroe, LA 71210
(318)387-1000 | FAX (318)387-1004

African American Investment Firms

Utendahl Capital Partners, L.P.
John O Utendahl, President & CEO
30 Broad Street 31st Floor
New York, NY 10004
(212)797-2500 | FAX (212)425-1866

Jackson Securities Inc.
Maynard H Jackson, Chairman & CEO
100 Peachtree St., NW Suite 2250
Atlanta, GA 30303
(404)522-5766 | FAX (404)524-1552

The Williams Capital Group, L.P.
Christopher J Williams, Pres. & CEO
650 Fifth Ave. 10th Floor
New York, NY 10019
(212)830-4500 | FAX (212)830-4575

First Commonwealth Securities Corp
Norbert A Simmons, President
201 St. Charles Avenue Suite 2500
New Orleans, LA 70170
(504)568-9377 | FAX (504)522-9124

Rice Financial Products Company.
J. Rice Jr., President & CEO
New York, NY
(212)432-7700 | FAX (212)432-7840

Siebert, Brandford, Shank & Co. LLC.
Suzanne F Shank, CEO
220 Sansome Street 15th Floor
San Francisco, CA 94104
(415)439-4450 | FAX (415)439-4480

M. R. Beal & Co.
Bernard B Beal, Chairman & CEO
565 Fifth Ave 8th Floor
New York, NY 10017
(212)983-3930 | FAX (212)983-4539

Blaylock & Partners, L.P.
Ronald E Blaylock, Chairman & CEO
609 Fifth Ave 12th Floor
New York, NY 10017
(212)715-6600 | FAX (212)754-4876

S.B.K. Brooks Investment Corp.
Eric L Small, President & CEO
824 Terminal Tower 50 Public Square
Cleveland, OH 44113
(216)861-6950 | FAX (216)861-7619

Powell Capital Markets, Inc.
Arthur F Powell, President
7 Becker Farm Road
Roseland, NJ 07068
(973)740-1230 | FAX (973)740-1787

Gilchrist & Company Inc
Harold Gilchrist, President
1732 Fifth Avenue North
Birmingham, AL 35203
(205)324-5231 | FAX (205)324-5234

The Chapman Company
Nathan A Chapman, President
401 East Pratt Street
Baltimore, MD 21202
(410)625-9656 | FAX (410)625-9313

Pryor, Counts & Co., Inc.
Malcolmn D Pryor, Chairman
1515 Market St. Suite 819
Philadelphia, PA 19102
(215)569-0274 | FAX (215)496-9109

Loop Capital Markets, LLC
James Reynolds Jr., Chairman & CEO
175 West Jackson Suite A635
Chicago, IL 60604
(312)913-4903 | FAX (312)913-4928

Walton Johnson & Company
Jesse McRae III, President
2711 North Haskell Ave. Suite 2070
Dallas, TX 75204
(214)821-3119 | FAX (214)821-3656

Harvestons Securities Inc.
Morgan Bassey President & CEo
Mile High Center 1700 Broadway Suite 412
Denver, CO 80290
(303)832-8887 | FAX (303)832-8882

Glossary of Common Terms

ABSTRACT OF TITLE A summarized history of the title of real property listing rights and liabilities such as easements, mortgages, liens, and transfers of title. The abstract gives evidence of the chain of title and whether or not the title is clear.

ACCELERATION CLAUSE A clause in a mortgage that provides, at the option of the lender, that the entire unpaid balance of the note would be due immediately upon failure to make a required payment or upon the sale of the property. In the latter case it is known as a due-on-sale acceleration clause. Usually it is found in paragraph 17 of a mortgage.

ACRE A quantity of land equal to 43,560 square feet. (For example, a square 208.7' x 208.7' or a rectangle 100' x 435.6).

ALL INCLUSIVE TRUST DEED The borrower obtains a new mortgage that is structured to include the old mortgage. The borrower makes payments on the new mortgage directly to the lender, who makes payments on the old first mortgage. (Also known as a Wrap-Around Mortgage.)

AMORTIZATION The reduction of debt over a fixed term on an installment basis.

AMORTIZED LOAN A loan in which the principal as well as the interest is payable in monthly or other periodic installments over the term of the loan.

ANNUITY A payment of equal installments paid periodically for a given number of periods.

APPRAISAL An estimation of value of real property "as of" the present or a past date (not future). Any of three methods are used where applicable: cost approach, income approach, and market data approach.

APPRAISER A disinterested party who evaluates a property and determines a value for it.

APPRAISED VALUE The value placed on a property by a qualified appraiser using one of several methods, i.e. replacement, comparison etc.

APPRECIATION Growth in value.

ARV After repair value

ASKING PRICE The price an appraiser has determined for a property and the price for which it is on the market.

ASSESSED VALUE The value placed on property by the taxing body of a county. This value is then used as a basis for computing taxes.

ASSESSMENTS A tax charge against real property by the taxing body of a county.

ASSET Any possession of value that an individual owns which may be used for payment of a debt.

ASSIGN To transfer one's rights in a bond, mortgage, lease, or other legal instrument to another person.

BIRD-DOG People who are on the lookout for properties that are for sale. Sometimes they earn a referral fee, if the property is purchased by an investor through their referrals.

BLANKET MORTGAGE One mortgage that covers several different parcels of real property.

BUYER'S BROKER A broker who represents the *buyer* when entering a real estate transaction. Generally, the *seller* pays the broker's commission at the closing.

CAPITAL Money used for investing purposes.

CAPITAL GAINS The profits realized above adjusted cost basis on the sale of property.

CASH FLOW Effective gross income minus operating expenses and debt service. (Also known as cash throw-off.)

CAVEAT EMPTOR Let the buyer beware. This statement does not apply where the buyer and seller are using an agent (broker).

CLOSING Sometimes called escrow, process by which title and monies of a property are transferred

CLOSING DATE A predetermined day that the transaction of buying/selling property will take place.

CONTINGENCY A possible event based on the happening of an uncertain future event.

CONTRACT A legal agreement entered by two or more parties which creates an agreement to do or not to do something.

CONTRACT FOR DEED A contract for the sale of real property wherein the seller is obligated to provide a merchantable title after the buyer has paid for the property, usually in installments. (Also known as an Agreement for Deed or Land Contract.)

CONTRACT FOR PURCHASE AND SALE An agreement between buyer and seller of real property to transfer title to that property at a future time for a specific sum of money. (Also called a sales contract).

CONVEYANCE An instrument (deed) legally sufficient to transfer title to real property.

COOPERATIVE An apartment house or similar property owned, usually in corporate form, by all the tenants. Each has stock in the corporation which owns the building.

COUNTER OFFER A change in price or terms of an unacceptable offer.

DEED An instrument conveying title to real property. It usually must be signed by the grantor (seller), witnessed by two persons, and recorded.

DISTRESSED PROPERTY A bargain property that is substantially below its present or projected renovated value.

DON'T WANTER Motivated seller for whatever reason

DP Down payment

DUPLEX A two-family home where the units share a common wall and are situated side by side.

EARNEST MONEY A deposit of money given by a party to bind the contract, usually credited toward the sales price.

EASEMENT An interest held by one party in the real property of another, giving that person the legal right to trespass on the other's property.

ENCROACHMENT An infringement, usually an improvement such as a building or fence, constructed on a property contiguous to the one infringing. An encroachment is usually revealed by a survey.

EQUITY In real estate, the value of an interest a person holds over and above any mortgages or liens on the property.

EQUITY OF REDEMPTION The right of a mortgagor (borrower) to buy back a property after a foreclosure sale. While equity of redemption does not exist in some states, in others it extends up to two years.

ESCAPE CLAUSE A clause added to the contract that allows either party the option of exiting the contract; thus, both parties are no longer bound by any contractual obligations.

ESCROW Money or documents held in trust by a neutral third party.

ESTATE Ownership interest in real property.

EXCULPATORY CLAUSE A clause in a contract relieving one of the parties of personal responsibility or liability. In a lease, the landlord is relieved of any responsibility for injury to tenants leasing his or her property. In a mortgage, the mortgagor (borrower) is relieved of any personal liability or deficiency judgment if a deficit occurs at a foreclosure sale.

EXECUTOR The administrator of an estate; one who is specified in the will.

FACE VALUE In reference to a note, the face value is the full amount for which the note has been written.

FAIR MARKET VALUE The appraised value of a property as compared with other property values on the market.

FLIPPING The turnover of property. An investor buys a property to immediately sell it for a profit.

FINANCIAL LEVERAGE The use of other peoples' money for investment purposes.

FINANCING The way in which an investor obtains the capital with which to purchase a property.

FIRST DEED OF TRUST A deed of trust recorded first. Equivalent to a first mortgage.

FLEXIBLE SELLER A seller who is willing to sell property in a nontraditional manner. This person may be flexible in terms, price, or both.

FORCED APPRECIATION A method of upping the value of a property through upgrades and repairs.

FORCED SALE The sale of a property used as security for a loan in order to repay creditor(s) in the event of a default on the loan.

FORECLOSURE The process whereby property pledged as security on a note is sold under court order because of default on the note.

135

GREATER FOOL THEORY Paying too much for a property and thinking you can find a fool who will pay even more.

INSTANT EQUITY The difference between the property's value and what you paid for it.

JOINT TENANCY A joint estate whereby upon the death of one joint tenant, his or her interest will go to the surviving joint tenant(s).

JOINT VENTURE An arrangement where two or more individuals or corporations join together on a single project as partners.

LAND TRUST A form of ownership whereby property is conveyed to a person or an institution, called a trustee, to be held and administered on behalf of another person called the beneficiary.

LB Lockbox

LEASE A contractual agreement between the owner (lessor) and the tenant (lessee), which allows the tenant the use and occupancy of the property for a specified period of time. A lease is an encumbrance against a title and gives the tenant an actual interest in the property known as an estate for years.

LEASE OPTION An agreement between two parties where the party who owns the property extends, to the second party, the right to purchase the property at a future date. The second party lives in the property until the lease option expires.

LETTER OF INTENT A letter stating a buyer's intent to make an offer to acquire a certain property. It is not a binding contract.

LIEN The right of a creditor to take and/or sell a property in the event of a default to satisfy the obligation of a debt.

LISTING BROKER A broker from the office which created the M.L.S. listing on a property.

LTV Loan to value

MECHANICS LIEN A lien right existing in favor of mechanics, suppliers, or other persons who have supplied materials or performed work in connection with the construction or repair of a building or other improvement.

MORTGAGE A temporary transfer of property to a creditor as collateral for a loan.

MORTGAGEE A lender of money under the terms of a mortgage.

MORTGAGOR The borrower, usually the owner, who pledges his or her property to assure performance in repaying the loan.

MULTIPLE LISTING SERVICE A multi-realty service whereby members of the local Board of Realtors exchange their listings.

NQNE Non-qualifying, non escalating

OPTION An instrument giving the right to a party to lease or purchase the property over a specified time period for a specified consideration. It is binding for the optionor (seller) but not the optionee (buyer).

OPTIONEE The person who has the legal right to purchase or not to purchase (through a contract) a specific property in the future.

OPTIONOR The seller of a property who extends an option to someone else. If the optionee exercises the option, this person is legally bound by the contractual obligations. However, if the option is not exercised, then the optionor is released from any responsibilities.

OWNERS OF RECORD All owners that are listed on a deed that is recorded in the county courthouse.

POINTS 1% of loan value

PURCHASE MONEY MORTGAGE A mortgage given to the seller as part or all of the consideration for the purchase of property. In effect, it is money loaned by the seller to the purchaser.

QUIT CLAIM DEED A deed transferring whatever interest in the property, if any, that the grantor may have. They are usually used to clear title.

R.E.O. (REAL ESTATE OWNED) Properties that financial institutions have repossessed as a result of a default on a mortgage and which these institutions are willing to sell.

REAL ESTATE AGENT A salesperson associated with a broker, who acts in behalf of a broker.

REALTOR A broker who is a member of the National Association of Realtors as well as state and local real estate boards.

RECORDING The act of entering, in the public record, any instrument affecting title to real property.

REDEMPTION The buying back of one's own property after a forced court sale. (See equity of redemption.)

RELEASE CLAUSE A statement in a blanket mortgage that allows a specific described parcel to be released from under the blanket lien after a sum of money is paid.

RENT CONTROL The regulation or restrictions set by government agencies on the amount of rent that landlords may charge.

SATISFACTION OF MORTGAGE An instrument filed in the public records which acknowledges payment of an indebtedness secured by a mortgage.

SECURITY DEPOSIT An amount of money paid by a tenant before moving into the premises to cover any damage incurred while living there, or to protect the landlord in the event that the tenant leaves without being current on rent payments. If the tenant is current and the unit only has a normal amount of wear and tear, then the deposit is generally refunded.

TAX SHELTER An income property that generates artificial paper losses, due to depreciation or cost recovery, that are in excess of the income produced by that property. These artificial losses can be used to offset other taxable income earned by the owners. In general, a tax shelter is any deferral, reduction, or elimination of a tax due.

TENANCY IN COMMON The ownership of an interest in property by two or more persons. Their ownership interest may be equal or unequal and there is no right of survivorship as with joint tenancy. The interest of any joint owner passes to his or her heirs or assigns after death.

TENANT A person having the temporary use and occupancy of real property owned by another.

TIME-SHARE A piece of property purchased by two or more parties who have set specific times when each may use or occupy the property.

TITLE INSURANCE Insurance issued by a title company guaranteeing the title to be good and marketable. Title insurance policies can be issued to protect the mortgagee only, the full interest of the buyer, or both.

TITLE INSURANCE COMPANY A business that reports on the status for the title on a specific property and whether or not it has any liens against it. After this title search has been completed, the company will issue a deed to be signed by all the owners of the property which should be notarized and recorded in the public records.

TOWNSHIP A unit of measure used in the government survey method of land description equal to 36 sections (36 square miles).

VACANCY RATE An estimate of the amount of time the rental property will be vacant (between tenants) multiplied by the rental rate of the unit(s). The amount is used in estimating the investor's value of an income property.

WRAPAROUND MORTGAGE A mortgage held by the seller-mortgagee. The buyer-mortgagor pays the seller-mortgagee the debt service on the wraparound mortgage and the seller-mortgagee continues to pay the debt service on the underlying or original mortgage.

YIELD Another term for interest

ZONING The laws which regulate and control for what the property may be used.

Index

About the Author

Larryette Kyle DeBose has over 22 years of real estate experience, including: holding Real Estate licenses in four states and selling commercial business properties. For more than fifteen years Ms. DeBose has been actively involved in real estate investing— tax properties, rehabs, foreclosures, restorations, rentals, and discounted notes.

Larryette Kyle DeBose has a Masters Degree in Public Administration (MPA) from the University Of Southern California (U.S.C). Ms. DeBose currently resides in Stone Mountain, Georgia and has one son.

For speaking engagements and questions, please contact:
Larryette Kyle DeBose
4828 Redan Rd #227
Stone Mountain, GA 30088
770-469-1595 Office
770-550-0333 Fax
lkdebose@aol.com
www.businessjumpstartseries.com

Special Thanks

—Dennis Kimbro, author, *Think & Grow Rich: A Black Choice*
(www.denniskimbro.com / dpkimbro@earthlink.net)

—Dr. Dorothy I. Height, President, of National Council of Negro Women
(www.ncnw.org / dheight@ncnw.org)

—Cynthia Franklin, Editor, The KIP Business Report
(www.kipbusinessreport.com / info@kipbusinessreport.com

—Ann Burns, Editor, *Library Journal*
www.libraryjournal.com

—Jesse B. Brown, Financial Guru, President/CEO-Krystal Investment Management
(www.investinthedream.com)

—Theresa Hall, Past President, Georgia Real Estate Investors Association
(tehall1028@aol.com)

Disclaimer

This publication is designed to provide accurate and authoritative information in regard to the subject matter covered. It is sold with the understanding that the author or publisher is not engaged in rendering legal, accounting or other professional service, If legal or other expert advise is required, the services of a competent professional person should be sought

L.K. DeBose

ORDER FORM

WWW.AMBERBOOKS.COM
African-American Self Help and Career Books

Fax Orders: 480-283-0991   Postal Orders: Send Checks & Money Orders to:
Telephone Orders: 480-460-1660   Amber Books Publishing
Online Orders: E-mail: Amberbks@aol.com   1334 E. Chandler Blvd., Suite 5-D67
                                       Phoenix, AZ 85048

____ *The African-American Guide to Real Estate Investing, $30,000 in 30 Days*
____ *The African-American Writer's Guide to Successful Self-Publishing*
____ *How to Be an Entrepreneur and Keep Your Sanity*
____ *Fighting for Your Life*
____ *The House that Jack Built*
____ *Langhorn & Mary: A 19th American Century Love Story*
____ *The African-American Woman's Guide to Great Sex, Happiness, & Marital Bliss*
____ *The Afrocentric Bride: A Style Guide*
____ *Beautiful Black Hair: A Step-by-Step Instructional Guide*
____ *How to Get Rich When You Ain't Got Nothing*
____ *The African-American Job Seeker's Guide to Successful Employment*
____ *The African-American Travel Guide*
____ *Suge Knight: The Rise, Fall, and Rise of Death Row Records*
____ *The African-American Teenagers Guide to Personal Growth, Health, Safety, Sex and Survival*
____ *Aaliyah—An R&B Princess in Words and Pictures*
____ *Wake Up and Smell the Dollars! Whose Inner City is This Anyway?*
____ *How to Own and Operate Your Home Day Care Business Successfully Without Going Nuts!*
____ *The African-American Woman's Guide to Successful Make-up and Skin Care*
____ *How to Play the Sports Recruiting Game and Get an Athletic Scholarship:*
____ *Is Modeling for You? The Handbook and Guide for the Young Aspiring Black Model*

Name:_____

Company Name:_____

Address:_____

City:_____ State:_____ Zip:_____

Telephone: (_____) _____E-mail:_____

For Bulk Rates Call: **480-460-1660**   # ORDER NOW

Real Estate Investing	$14.95		Successful Make-up	$14.95
Successful Self-Publishing	$14.95		Sports Recruiting:	$12.95
How to be an Entrepreneur	$14.95		Modeling:	$14.95
Fighting for Your Life	$14.95			
The House That Jack Built	$16.95		❑ Check ❑ Money Order ❑ Cashiers Check	
Langhorn & Mary	$25.95		❑ Credit Card: ❑ MC ❑ Visa ❑ Amex ❑ Discover	
Great Sex	$14.95		CC#_____	
The Afrocentric Bride	$16.95			
Beautiful Black Hair	$16.95		Expiration Date:_____	
How to Get Rich	$14.95		**Payable to:**	
Job Seeker's Guide	$14.95		Amber Books	
Travel Guide	$14.95		1334 E. Chandler Blvd., Suite 5-D67	
Suge Knight	$21.95		Phoenix, AZ 85048	
Teenagers Guide	$19.95			
Aaliyah	$10.95		**Shipping:** $5.00 per book. Allow 7 days for delivery.	
Wake Up & Smell the Dollars	$18.95		**Sales Tax:** Add 7.05% to books shipped to Arizona addresses.	
Home Day Care	$12.95			
			Total enclosed: $_____	

loose pages
repaired
2/17
RC